Your Inner Dog

Diane Morgan

Your Inner Dog

Project Team
Editor: Stephanie Fornino
Copy Editor: Joann Woy
Indexer: Lucie Haskins
Design: Stephanie Krautheim and Mary Ann Kahn
Illustrations: Stephanie Krautheim

T.F.H. Publications
President/CEO: Glen S. Axelrod
Executive Vice President: Mark E. Johnson
Publisher: Christopher T. Reggio
Production Manager: Kathy Bontz

T.F.H. Publications, Inc.
One TFH Plaza
Third and Union Avenues
Neptune City, NJ 07753

Printed and bound in China
08 09 10 11 12   1 3 5 7 9 8 6 4 2

Library of Congress Cataloging-in-Publication Data
Morgan, Diane, 1947-
    Your inner dog : discover what your favorite breed says about you / Diane Morgan.
        p. cm.
    Includes index.
    ISBN 978-0-7938-0659-1 (alk. paper)
    1. Dogs. 2. Dogs--Selection. 3. Dog breeds. I. Title.
    SF426.M6794 2008
    636.7--dc22

                    2008017663

This book has been published with the intent to provide accurate and authoritative information in regard to the subject matter within. While every reasonable precaution has been taken in preparation of this book, the author and publisher expressly disclaim responsibility for any errors, omissions, or adverse effects arising from the use or application of the information contained herein. The techniques and suggestions are used at the reader's discretion and are not to be considered a substitute for veterinary care. If you suspect a medical problem, consult your veterinarian.

The information within is not meant to replace serious breed research, help you find a compatible dog breed, or be in any way predictive of future events. Also, all advice given is for entertainment purposes only and should not be considered fact.

The Leader In Responsible Animal Care For Over 50 Years!®
www.tfh.com

Table of Contents

Introduction

Why do we choose the dogs we do? Or why do they choose us? Sometimes it's just happenstance—you saw a dog who needed to be rescued and adopted him. Sometimes breed choice is driven by practical considerations—while you may passionately desire to own a Border Collie, for instance, a Chihuahua may suit your lifestyle better. More often, however, there seems to be some powerful mystical attraction that draws us together, something not based on physical appearance or even lifestyle. It goes much deeper—to the magical place where spirit meets spirit. Some breeds seem to draw owners whose characteristics mirror their own. Others seem to attract a complementary soul. It's really just like a relationship: Sometimes like attracts like, and sometimes opposites go for each other.

This book represents what I have learned during decades of dog and people watching. Some of it comes from my own observations, some from interviews with dog owners, and some from just hunch and intuition. And more than one dog I know let me in on a few family secrets.

What follows is a lighthearted look at the various factors that go into making us who we are, based on our favorite dog breeds: personality and character traits, hobbies, fashion choices, favorite foods, lucky numbers, pet peeves, and more. Just remember, it's all in fun and not meant to replace serious breed research.

How This Book Works

Your Inner Dog profiles 75 types of people based on the dog breeds they own or love. The profiles are further divided into five major groups: Pretty and Polished, Fit and Fun, Valiant and Vivacious, Smart and Sassy, and Cultured and Classic. Within these chapter groupings, individual breed types feature the following categories:

Personality and Character: This section reveals your inner self—the traits that make you the wonderful, mysterious individual that you are.

Best Trait: Everybody has at least one superior attribute. If you don't know what yours is yet, this section will clue you in!

Your Space: We all need a special place to call our own, whether it's a gleaming, ultramodern chrome kitchen or a comfortable, shabby-chic living room. Find out where your Shangri-la is.

Career: We can't all be rocket scientists, but your breed choice says more than you might suspect about where you may flourish in the job market.

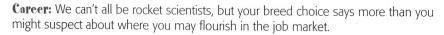

Leisure Time and Entertainment: Are you a movie buff or an art aficionado? A dancer or a hiker? What vacation destinations are calling your name? Find out here!

Fashion Musts: High heels or sneakers? Ralph Lauren or Gucci? This section reveals your sense of style and makes some suggestions on how to put together your most flattering look.

Food Faves: Some of us like fast food, others gourmet specialties. Vegetarians, meat eaters, and exotic food lovers lurk among us. Who are they? Discover what your taste buds yearn for right here.

Pet Peeves: Whether it's gum snapping or people without a sense of humor, everyone has a pet peeve. Find out yours.

Significant Others: Who's your perfect mate? Which characteristics should you be looking for, and which should you avoid? You may be surprised!

Other Compatible Dogs: Don't just limit yourself to one breed profile! This section lists other breeds with whom you might also be compatible, meaning the correlating personality profile for each will mesh with your own.

Lucky Number: In the numerological system used here, each letter of your breed's full name is assigned a number from one to nine—based on the ancient Pythagorean system—and added together in a special way to reveal your lucky number.

Notable Breed People: You stand in the company of greatness, whether it's a famous historical figure, actor, athlete, designer, writer, musician, or dancer. Find out who else owns or has owned your favorite breed, and decide if you have anything in common.

If you don't recognize yourself in a particular category, don't worry. Sooner or later, you'll develop a taste for sushi, a yen to visit Labrador, or a passion for heavy metal.

How to Use This Book

Using this book is fun and easy—simply take the ten-question quiz featured on page 6. Your answers will direct you to a chapter, where you'll find lots of breed profiles that suit you best. You can also just look up your favorite breed or breeds and start reading! Use the "Other Compatible Breed Personalities" section of your chosen profile to help you find even more breed profiles to match your personality. Above all, have fun!

Quiz
What Breed Personality Are You?

Directions: To find out which breed personalities most closely match your own, take this ten-question quiz, choosing the letter of the response that suits you best. Add up your answers and see pages 8 and 9—you will be directed to a specific chapter, where you'll find lots of compatible breed personality profiles.

When you're having a bad day, you:
- a. Shop till you drop—a new pair of Jimmy Choos and suddenly all is right with the world!
- b. Know that your spinning class will make you forget all about it.
- c. Confront whatever seems to be causing the problem and try to work it out.
- d. Call all your friends and analyze, in great detail, whatever happened to upset you.
- e. Make a cocktail and take a nice bubble bath—you know things will be better tomorrow.

2. Your driving style could be described as:
- a. A bit distracted. How better to apply lip gloss than by using the rearview mirror?
- b. Fast and furious. The highway is your racetrack, and you can't understand why everyone else is driving so slowly!
- c. Assertive. The left lane is your domain—and while some may accuse you of tailgating, you like to think of it as "cozying up with fellow drivers."
- d. Efficient. You can't remember the last time you got lost—you have your route planned out way before it's time to leave the house.
- e. Considerate. You never forget to use your turn signal and have pulled over more than once to assist a motorist in need.

3. If you were at a party and didn't know anyone, you would:
- a. Zero in on the best-dressed person there and ask where they got their outfit.
- b. Ask the buff redhead "What gym do you go to?"
- c. Attack the appetizers and hope that no one tries to talk to you while your mouth is full.
- d. Attempt to impress the other guests with your knowledge of ancient Roman warfare.
- e. Drop off your perfect hostess gift (thank you, Martha Stewart), then survey the room and subtly integrate yourself into the party.

4. In high school, you were voted:
- a. Most likely to star in an off-Broadway musical.
- b. Most likely to win the New York marathon.
- c. Most likely to climb Mount Everest.
- d. Most likely to invent a new "green" fuel source.
- e. Most likely to be invited to the White House.

5. If you were stranded on a deserted island, you couldn't do without your:
- a. Hair dryer and makeup kit—after all, you never know who'll be rescuing you!
- b. Stairmaster and "Sweatin' to the Oldies" tapes—nobody cheers you up like Richard Simmons.

c. Swiss Army knife—finally, 99 out of the 100 features will actually come in handy.

d. Copy of Homer's *Iliad*—now you won't have to pretend you've read it.

e. Classical music collection—you can conduct the palm trees and native birds in Beethoven's 5th.

6. At a costume party, you'd likely be wearing:

a. A fairy princess costume. Lots of glitter and a tiara are necessary accessories, of course.

b. A superhero costume—you know you can pull off that spandex unitard like nobody's business.

c. A Darth Vader cloak and mask. You can finally put your dead-on "Luke, I am your father" impression to good use!

d. Your own clothes—costume parties are silly!

e. A traditional masquerade mask, a dark cape, and some Mardi Gras beads—but you'd keep it classy, of course.

7. When it comes to relationship advice, you'd be comfortable seeking it from:

a. The Psychic Friends Network—99 cents a minute buys some sage advice.

b. Your personal trainer—he knows how to get you six-pack abs and when to eighty-six a loser.

c. Oprah. Enough said.

d. Your shrink, even though she counters every question with "What do *you* think?"

e. Your parents. Even if Mom ends up muttering about grandkids, they still know best.

8. If you won the lottery, you would:

a. Did somebody say makeover?!

b. Start your own company—perhaps a gym with attached smoothie shop.

c. Take a permanent vacation jet-setting around the globe.

d. Put all the money in the bank and save it—no crazy splurges for you!

e. Give most of the money to charity, friends, and family, then spend a little something on yourself.

9. Your idea of the perfect day involves:

a. A relaxing, pampering-filled day at the spa.

b. Running in a marathon and finishing in record time.

c. Swimming with sharks off a coral reef somewhere in the Caribbean.

d. Catching up on a good book while lying in a hammock.

e. Wine tasting at your favorite vineyard.

10. If you were a style of dance, you would be:

a. Ballet.

b. Belly dance.

c. Street dance.

d. Modern dance.

e. Ballroom dance.

Mostly A's
Pretty and Polished

Charm…beauty…social graces…joie de vivre…elegance. You have it all, you know you have it all, and you want everybody else to know you have it all, too. And "it" includes the cutest dog on the block. See Chapter 1: Pretty and Polished to find a profile that matches you best.

Mostly B's
Fit and Fun

Run! Climb! Jump! Dive! Keep moving, keep laughing, and keep having a blast—that's what life is all about for you sportin' dog owners. Your dogs are not just your pets but your friends, companions, and heart of hearts. See Chapter 2: Fit and Fun to find a profile that matches you best.

Your Inner Dog

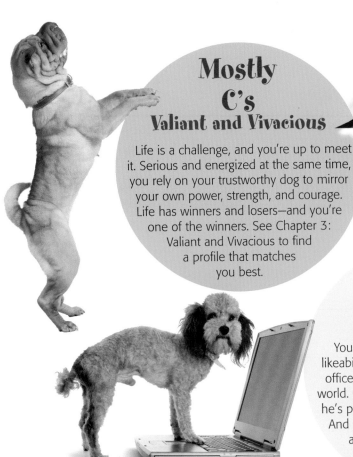

Mostly C's
Valiant and Vivacious

Life is a challenge, and you're up to meet it. Serious and energized at the same time, you rely on your trustworthy dog to mirror your own power, strength, and courage. Life has winners and losers—and you're one of the winners. See Chapter 3: Valiant and Vivacious to find a profile that matches you best.

Mostly D's
Smart and Sassy

Your intelligence is daunting, but your likeability factor is just as high, so run for office, start a business, or take over the world. Only don't forget your dog because he's probably smarter than most people. And so are you. See Chapter 4: Smart and Sassy to find a profile that matches you best.

Mostly E's
Cultured and Classic

You treasure all the values of life, including art, beauty, fine cuisine, and love. With your rich and complex character, you are a mystery to many but not to your faithful friend. He at least understands you—and the importance of good literature. See Chapter 5: Cultured and Classic to find a profile that matches you best.

Chapter 1
Pretty and Polished

Bichon Frise People • Brussels Griffon People • Cairn Terrier People •

Cavalier King Charles Spaniel People • Chihuahua People •

Chinese Crested People • French Bulldog People • Italian Greyhound People

• Maltese People • Papillon People • Pekingese People •

Pomeranian People • Pug People •

Shih-Tzu People • Yorkshire Terrier People

Bichon Frise People

Personality and Character: You are a success in life, and that success is well deserved—indeed, you have earned everything you have. You are growth-oriented and have tremendous mental resources, although you tend to be somewhat conservative, at least outwardly, and perhaps overly intellectual. You take a great deal of time and effort with your work. (This is clearly apparent in the care you take of your dog's beautiful coat.) If you are interested in something, you can do it. You have a real talent for amassing wealth, although you tend to be somewhat conservative in your investments, and curiously enough, are not particularly interested in money for its own sake. Far more important to you is what you can do with it. And for you, that means using it to further important causes, particularly environmental issues. You care a great deal for the environment and all its denizens, a concern that manifests itself in every aspect of your life. Your passion is to make a real difference in the world.

Best Trait: You are able to make anything you do a success.

Your Space: You have a very bold, classic sense of design, and you are not afraid of using simple colors, with brash red and orange for accents. You're really good at wallpapering, especially with those new textile fabrics. You also love tile and use it liberally in your home. (Tile comes in handy when there's that little doggy accident now and then.) You are picky about the lamps—you love the Tiffany touch. Your kitchen is airy, organized, streamlined, and simple.

Career: You would make a good healer, either as a doctor or a dentist.

Leisure Time and Entertainment: Walking, bicycling, cooking, stamp collecting, and writing. One of your favorite artists is Louis-Eugéne Lambert, the French painter who painted such a wonderful portrait of a Bichon Frise, now in the American Kennel Club (AKC) museum collection.

As far as vacation is concerned, you like to travel to places like Nice, Portugal, or Morocco—something around the Mediterranean, the original homeland of your dog. You also take your dog everywhere you go; luckily, Bichons are pretty portable.

Fashion Musts: Bichon Frise people look great in flowing tunic tops, along with long, beaded necklaces. Silk is your best fabric. And get a shoulder bag! For outerwear, a belted, hip-length jacket is just right for you. Your best color is silver. You love glamorous designers like Fendi and Valentino.

Food Faves: Sweet potato pie (in fact, any kind of pie) and Chinese takeout are favorites. You like ham sandwiches and pork barbecue as well.

You love to drive, and you are quite good at it.

Pet Peeves: Inefficiency and disorganization are your biggest pet peeves.

Significant Others: You take your love life very seriously, and you don't usually go against your instincts when it comes to potential partners. While you are generally easy to get along with, you can react with anger when you get pushed too far. Look for someone who is very easygoing.

Other Compatible Breed Personalities: Besides the Bichon Frise, you are compatible with American Staffordshire Terriers and Collies.

Lucky Number: Numerological calculations for your breed reveal your lucky number to be 9.

Notable Bichon People: Kathy Lee Gifford, Sidney and Claire Pollack, Barbra Streisand, Betty White

Brussels Griffon People

Personality and Character: You have a mind of your own and are not afraid to use it. You also have a good deal of curiosity and intelligence, and you love to learn. However, you prefer not to lead and can sometimes make poor choices about whom to follow. Once in a while, you have a habit of turning a simple conversation into a confrontation (you don't mean to—it just happens), but most of the time you have a good perspective on life. You are known for being sensitive and very kind. You tend to take yourself pretty seriously, but you have a really comical side to you, even if you're not always aware of it. It would be to your benefit to learn to mix work and play a little more freely.

Best Trait: Your kindness is your best trait.

Your Space: You desire a combination of elegance and comfort and like to use a little feng shui to get it. Your kitchen is almost like a living room—it has plenty of comfortable chairs and even a television. It is a secure, stable, and traditional place, reflecting the values you hold yourself. You are a pretty good cook as well—you have a real way with those brussels sprouts, or at least would if you could stand them!

Career: You don't feel comfortable in jobs that require a lot of theory or conceptual analysis but would do well in health care, library science, or in a business of your own.

Leisure Time and Entertainment: You have wonderful abilities as a climber (social and

otherwise), and by all means you should exercise them. You have cosmopolitan taste when it comes to literature and the arts, and you like anything that is new and interesting. You also love jazz and blues. When it comes to movies, you like romantic comedies, especially *As Good as It Gets*, which features your breed. The *Star Wars* series is also a favorite—the Ewoks in *The Return of the Jedi* are said to resemble Brussels Griffons, but frankly, you can't see the resemblance. Or can you? For vacation, a nice trip to Belgium, the homeland of your dog, might be enjoyable. However, when you're done there, you might consider a trip to the Alps or back home to the Rockies—your love of climbing makes them perfect destinations for you.

Fashion Musts: When it comes to fashion, just as with your home decor, you like elegant pieces that are also comfortable. For a modern, tailored look, try a Kenneth Cole skirt and button-up shirt for work—you'll look sophisticated but approachable. Top it off with a great pair of chunky heels and maybe a short beaded or pearl necklace. Your eyes are one of your best features, so try maximizing them with a contrasting eye shadow and dark mascara.

Food Faves: Not even you really like brussels sprouts, but you pretend to, for the sake of your beloved dog's name. Belgian fries, waffles, and chocolate are much more to your liking—especially the chocolate. You also enjoy experimenting with interesting teas, like chai and rooibos.

Significant Others: You need someone with a high social intelligence who can understand you and your deep need for tenderness. You are not afraid of being vulnerable, although you should probably put up a bit more of a guard. Learn to let bygones be bygones, and stop trying to get even.

Other Compatible Breed Personalities: Besides the Brussels Griffon, you are compatible with Borzoi and Jack Russell Terriers.

Pet Peeve: You don't like it when people lie—even a white lie.

Lucky Number: Numerological calculations for your breed reveal your lucky number to be 1.

Notable Brussels Griffon People: Kevin Sorbo, Queen Astrid of Belgium

Pretty and Polished

Personality and Character: You are easygoing, neither pushy nor subservient. What is really delightful about you is that you generally look at the positive side of things. Indeed, you are a child at heart—you even still enjoy your afternoon nap! You do have a biting wit when the occasion calls for it. You are always in the mood for fun adventures and are known for being both funny and irreverent. You love a schedule and have a tendency to become stressed when things get out of hand. (The naps help.) For better or worse, however, most people don't even know when you are stressed—you are good at hiding things under your quiet, no-nonsense demeanor. Your best trait is your honesty, but it's also your worse trait. You can be brutally frank, and sometimes what you think is "constructive criticism" can offend.

Best Trait: Your wit is your best trait.

Your Space: Like your rock-loving dog ("cairn" means a pile of rocks, you know), you enjoy the strength and power of stone. Your signature tree is the pine tree (it's as strong and tough as you are)—think about planting one on your property, along with a giant boulder or two, to declare your allegiance to rocks.

Career: Consider counseling, psychoanalysis, or working in a luxury trade. You are one who can work overtime without complaint, as long as the benefits are generous. In any case, look for a job with a great deal of stability. You are not in the least shy and wouldn't mind a job that involves public speaking.

Leisure Time and Entertainment: You love talking on the phone, singing (your voice is really great), reading, writing, jogging (with a partner), and roller skating. You enjoy mingling with a sporting crowd and have a secret love for hockey and indoor football. Your favorite movie is *The Wizard of Oz*, of course. (One of the world's most famous Cairns, Toto, is one of the main attractions!) You also keep up with celebrity gossip, perhaps more than you should. One of your favorite television shows is *American Idol*, where you can enjoy the antics of fellow Cairn Terrier lover Simon Cowell. (You are more like him than you want to admit!)

   Since you've already been to Oz, there's not much left in terms of vacation. But you might try visiting the Netherlands—it is so completely un-Ozlike that you might find it refreshing.

Fashion Musts: Physically, your best trait is your enviable figure. You may be tempted now and again to color your hair, but you don't really need to, you know. Like the Cairn Terrier himself, you look great in all colors. Whatever you wear is chic and appropriate. You look especially great in tailored jackets and jeans. Emeralds are a good accessory for you. Try Some draped, fitted separates by designer Lloyd Klein.

Food Faves: Poultry for dinner and peanut butter pie for dessert! When you want to get more complicated, you like decadent treats like blue cheesecake with a walnut shortbread crust, pears, and port glace. And beer at any time—that's one reason you're always on a diet.

Significant Others: You gravitate toward people with healthy habits—to help keep you on track. And of course, you are attracted to people with brains (like the Scarecrow), heart (like the Tin Man), and courage (like the Lion). You like people with a thin or medium build, and you tend to go for younger types—that's fine because they are attracted to you as well.

Other Compatible Breed Personalities: Besides Cairn Terriers, you are compatible with Fox Terriers and Pomeranians.

Pet Peeve: You hate tornadoes.

Lucky Number: Numerological calculations for your breed reveal your lucky number to be 3.

Notable Cairn People: Simon Cowell, Dorothy Gale, Liza Minnelli, James Woods

Cavalier King Charles Spaniel People

Personality and Character: Imperturbable, debonair, and original, your watchwords are peace and harmony. You are extremely hospitable, friendly, and welcoming to others; indeed, no one can come within a block of your house without being plied with offers of food and drink. Pleasure is your middle name, and you are inspired by art and beauty. You have the unique ability to turn a disastrous day or week into a wonderful adventure by the sheer force of your easygoing charm—you just don't allow things to get too bad. You don't like abstract theory unless you can see a practical application. You are fascinated by other people, whether they're everyday folks or celebrities. You've been accused of being nosy, but honestly, you are just interested in things, especially politics.

Best Trait: You have an extremely easygoing nature.

Your Space: If you are a suburbanite, you enjoy tending to your perfectly manicured lawn. You dislike anything that is scruffy, and that includes your dog. The accoutrements to your home reflect your simple yet cosmopolitan taste: abstract vases, bamboo rugs, and Bombay double-drawer chests. And a beautiful aluminum sundial for your lawn.

Career: You excel at anything involving critical thinking and intellectual stimulation, such as teaching or writing. It should be said, however, that your attitude toward work can be. . . well. . . cavalier. However, while you resent being asked to work overtime, you produce more in a few hours than most people do in a week. You also work very well under pressure.

Leisure Time and Entertainment: You are drawn to historical novels, especially those detailing the life of King Charles I. In your more romantic moments, nothing but *Romeo and Juliet* will suffice. And of course, the Cavalier poets are among your favorites, especially Richard Lovelace. You also enjoy talk shows, like *Larry King Live* and *The Oprah Winfrey Show*—you learn the most amazing things from those shows!

For a vacation, try a historical tour of Merrie Olde England, seeing all the great Cavalier sights, including the Tower of London.

Fashion Musts: You fare well in dramatic makeup and flowing clothes with high heels. You appreciate hand-knit clothes like those made by designer Micha King. You like to wear precious gemstones, especially rubies (one of the possible colors of your Cavalier's hair). Speaking of which, be careful not to use too much heat on your hair—you'll ruin it. (It can be flyaway, but there are better ways of controlling it.)

Food Faves: You're not too picky in the food department, as long as a good wine is served. You do have a fondness for chili peppers. You have a weakness for chocolate, although you also appreciate a good almond tart.

Significant Others: If you suspect that a relationship is failing, you can become irrationally jealous. You may have had to deal with a number of romantic rejections. You enjoy civilized people who treat you with you all the gallantry, courtesy, and attention you deserve. You yourself are absolutely faithful to your significant other, never straying even in thought, as was said of King Charles I himself.

Other Compatible Breed Personalities: Besides the Cavalier, you are compatible with German Shorthaired Pointers and Italian Greyhounds.

Pet Peeve: You hate that shabby old leather armchair your significant other refuses to get rid of because the dog likes it.

Lucky Number: Numerological calculations for your breed reveal your lucky number to be 2.

Notable Cavalier People: Lauren Bacall, Courteney Cox, Ronald Reagan, Diane Sawyer, Frank Sinatra, Liv Tyler

Personality and Character: Those who first meet you are struck by your strong sense of personal dignity, and your love of virtue is clearly apparent. You have a true concern for the way others think and feel, and you are protective and nurturing of them—yet you are sometimes (wisely) cynical of the motives of others. When people know you better and earn your trust, they become aware of the bubbly—even effervescent—side of your nature. Chihuahua owners also have an extraordinary vision of the way things should be. You can be prone to sudden little fits of temper, but you're unlikely to do anything that generates conflict; in fact, you dislike conflict intensely. You are a wanderer in spirit, if not always in fact.

Best Trait: You are an idealist, a trait that many people admire.

Your Space: In the city, you're often seen skulking around museums and art galleries. Chihuahua owners who live in the country tend to stay there, however, seldom venturing out into urban areas. The morning is your favorite time of day. As to your home's style, you're partial to the shabby-chic trend, old chandeliers and all. You'd even like to get a pink one, but you get enough flak when you paint your dog's toenails pink.

Career: Some Chihuahua people make great inventors and criminal lawyers. Others go into social work, gardening, and child care to fulfill their nurturing urge. (This may be one reason why you are drawn to the tiny, puppy-like Chihuahua in the first place.) Still others of you give in to your money-making side and go into bond trading. Chihuahua people are very suited to executive positions of all types. (Their tact helps them gain the promotion.)

Leisure Time and Entertainment: You love biking, sentimental love songs, and parties. You also write poetry when you can find the time. You like card games, such as poker, and are quite good at them. You also enjoy contemporary art, like the portrait of Chihuahua Ch. Kay's Don Feleciano-L, painted by Roy Andersen.

As an essentially conservative person, you're not that anxious to roam too far. In fact, nothing beats a quiet summer afternoon in the backyard. If you do leave the area and wish to remain true to your breed, however, there's no place like Chihuahua, Mexico. It has everything—at least if you like mountains and cactus deserts.

Fashion Musts: You like subtle makeup, although sometimes you add a dramatic touch, such as dark lipstick or a smoky eye shadow. You were born for diamond earrings. Classic designers, like Ralph Lauren, are your favorites.

Food Faves: Well, of course you like Mexican foods, and you *love* Mexican beer as well. But you are also a connoisseur of cheese and tea, although you also enjoy a good burger or taco. For dessert, you like cheesecake with whipped cream and chocolate-covered coffee beans.

Significant Others: You are deeply affectionate—to the point of self-sacrifice. You fall in love easily, and rejection is extraordinarily painful to you. Making hasty decisions about your love life can be disastrous!

Other Compatible Breed Personalities: Besides Chihuahuas, you are compatible with Afghan Hounds and Pekingese.

Pet Peeve: You hate bad art.

Lucky Number: Numerological calculations for your breed reveal your lucky number to be 8.

Notable Chihuahua People: Paula Abdul, Hilary Duff, Paris Hilton, Madonna, Demi Moore, Britney Spears

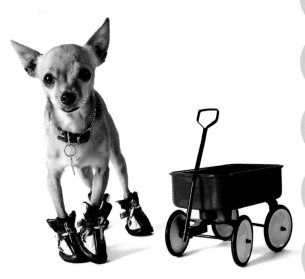

Personality and Character: You are a true original and a great visionary. A natural leader and pioneer, you can also work well on a team, where you are usually the most productive member. In fact, you don't like being alone. Athletic, creative, and impulsive, your restless energy lets you accomplish many things—like thinking up new inventions! You possess the gifts of subtle persuasion and undeniable charm. You enjoy the public spotlight—when called to center stage, you perform beautifully. You also tend to be somewhat materialistic and status conscious; indeed, you find it hard to stay attached to either people or places for any length of time.

Best Trait: You have a lot of creative energy.

Your Space: You love the dining room at home. You feel that this room is overlooked by too many people—forsaken for the kitchen and the den—and you have a mission to restore it to its former state of glory. You like a winding staircase and will always have your own flower and herb garden. However, you don't have an irretrievable attachment to any one place.

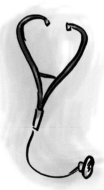

Career: You could have a brilliant career in science, the arts, medicine, or law. You're a dedicated worker—the kind of person who would learn Italian just to read Dante's works in the original. In some ways, you are a rather high-maintenance employee—but you're worth the trouble.

Leisure Time and Entertainment: You like fantasy and adventure novels, such as the *Harry Potter* series. As a child, you were mesmerized by the adventures of Robin Hood and always had a soft spot for classics like *David Copperfield* and *Ivanhoe*. You also enjoy bridge, sculpting, writing poetry, arty movies, watching television, and listening to music.

For vacation, let your adventurous spirit roam—explore the Amazon, climb Mount Everest, or visit the pyramids of Egypt. You also enjoy a good cruise, where you can catch up on your sleep.

Fashion Musts: Blue is a great color for you, but you are so incandescent that you can light up any outfit. You look great in structured cotton jackets for a casual yet tailored look. When you go out, don't underestimate the power of the little black dress! Subtly sophisticated designers like Yves St. Laurent appeal to you.

Food Faves: You love dining out, where you show off your highly discriminating palate: smoked trout mousse, steak in flaky pastry, apple pie crepes. And you like your wine. At home, your taste runs to sweet snacks, especially pies.

Significant Others: You need a partner who is dedicated, strong—and as smart as you are. Impulsive Chinese Crested people should work on choosing the perfect mate carefully. You tend to flee from relationships for no clear reason.

Other Compatible Breed Personalities: Beside Chinese Cresteds, you are compatible with designer dogs and Lhasa Apsos.

Pet Peeve: You don't like dull people.

Lucky Number: Numerological calculations for your breed reveal your lucky number to be 2.

Notable Chinese Crested People: Danny Bonaduce, Amanda Bynes, Cruella De Vil, Gypsy Rose Lee

Personality and Character: Although you may have had some setbacks when you were younger, you overcame them. When you think about your life now, you know that you have many things to be thankful for, including your home and your treasured friends. Most of the time you are peaceful and quiet, and you really prefer staying home with your family to going out. You are a person of fierce convictions, and you know who you are. Your character is set—and has been since childhood. You have a deep sense of life's purpose. You like to do your own thing, but you can be overly self-conscious and somewhat pessimistic. This may be a result of your brooding attention to psychology, aesthetics, and self-analysis. You are a workaholic and a factual encyclopedia—you're good with names, dates, and other trivia, amazing people with your knowledge. You love peace and harmony, but you do tend to isolate yourself at times—you especially like solitary hobbies such as working on your car. Still, you are a very thoughtful person—the kind who creates custom gift baskets for no special reason at all. That is why people love you.

Best Trait: Your self-awareness is your best trait.

Your Space: Sometimes, it's under your truck. Other times, it's your beanbag chair. You're also pretty fond of the bathroom, kitchen (which is huge), and study. You are definitely the stay-at-home type, and you prefer a traditional, classic look. In fact, if you had your way, your house would be so traditional that it would come with turrets and a moat. You certainly have no objection to used furniture, either. You might enjoy putting in a white garden.

Your Inner Dog

Career: Something in television, perhaps as a host or researcher, might suit you best. You would also do well in any field that calls upon you to be a master of trivia.

Leisure Time and Entertainment: You enjoy skateboarding, newspapers, magazines, collecting things, and gardening. You also enjoy classic pop music artists like the Beatles and Madonna. You like to read reference books and have largely memorized the *Farmer's Almanac*, the dictionary, and *Everything You Always Wanted to Know About Sex but Were Afraid to Ask*. You even have a sort of affinity to Hamlet; you understand him, even if no one else does.

For vacation, you enjoy warm-weather places that afford lots of opportunity for long walks and communion with nature. (A cruise is definitely out.)

Fashion Musts: At home, you like casual (but well-made) clothes, like fitted T-shirts and turtleneck sweaters. In the real world, you are fond of expensive, soft fabrics. (You're a little bit of a label snob and know that good things never really go out of style.) You love classic sportswear designers like Calvin Klein. You do best in dark or muted colors like brown, beige, and khaki. Dark red is also a possibility. Silver goes well with your lifestyle—so does citrine or yellow sapphires.

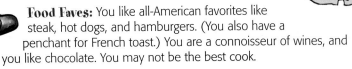

Food Faves: You like all-American favorites like steak, hot dogs, and hamburgers. (You also have a penchant for French toast.) You are a connoisseur of wines, and you like chocolate. You may not be the best cook.

Significant Others: You like simple dates—just walking around or sitting by a fountain and holding hands. Your significant other never has to worry about you straying, that's for sure. With those you love, you are strong and comforting, if somewhat obsessive.

Other Compatible Breed Personalities: Besides French Bulldogs, you are compatible with Bullmastiffs and Rottweilers.

Pet Peeve: People who ask for too many details—and that includes people at airport security. You always seem to be the one they pick on to unpack everything in your suitcase.

Lucky Number: Numerological calculations for your breed reveal your lucky number to be 1.

Notable French Bulldog People: Jason Priestly, Martha Stewart, Reese Witherspoon

Personality and Character: You have a deep sense of life's purpose and exude self-confidence and a sense of tranquility most of the time. Your outward calmness masks a steel core—it is this same core of steel you find in your dog. You are gentle, friendly, kind, and generous. Still, there is a certain sense of remoteness about you, a sense of polite restraint. You dislike being bound by obligations. Most of the time you are peaceful and quiet, and you really prefer staying home with your family to going out. Still, you shine in company. You can talk entertainingly of books; in fact, you are somewhat of a literary gossip. You are also a very thoughtful person—the kind who sends the perfect gift for no special reason at all. You are very adept at getting exactly what you want—and can be persistent about it until it happens. (What you want often has to do with money.) You are perfectly capable of putting those who do not give in on a guilt trip.

Best Traits: Your best traits are your great sense of humor and exquisite taste.

Your Space: Your living room—you like accents of white and gold. You also love your bedroom, especially lounging around in bed on rainy mornings. (Italian Greyhounds are not crazy about rain.) You love to change the furniture around, but you leave it to others to fix the leaky ceilings.

Career: You would do very well in a field where you can work from home—perhaps as a writer of self-help books. Whatever you do, you do it well and conscientiously.

Leisure Time and Entertainment: You like golfing, climbing, and cook-offs. You also enjoy the opera (Italian, of course) and concerts. Indeed, you enjoy music of all sorts. You are a great reader of everything, and you are quite good at needlework. Some of your favorite artists include Giotto and Hieronymus Bosch, both of whom painted your favorite breed.

For vacation, there's nothing like a gondola ride in Venice, is there? You also might enjoy a cross-country trip, especially if you can do it in an RV rather than stay in strange hotels.

Fashion Musts: You look great in white and fabrics with a sheen to them—and just go right ahead and wear that tiara. You love emeralds set with diamonds in antique gold. However, there is another fashion side to you. Just as your dog is part toy and part athlete, there is a dynamic, sporty side to you as well. This is the side that wears hiking boots, jeans, and sandals, without jewelry or makeup. For comfortable pieces that employ really beautiful fabrics, try something by Donna Karan.

Food Faves: You understand good food and good wine, but a cup of really good chocolate is heaven to you. You really enjoy picnics (with good bread and red wine) with your family and friends.

Significant Others: Family ties are sacred to you. You dislike drama scenes and emotional roller coasters. A calm and secure relationship is a must for you.

Other Compatible Breed Personalities: Besides Italian Greyhounds, you are compatible with Cavalier King Charles Spaniels and German Shorthaired Pointers.

Pet Peeve: You dislike mean-spirited practical jokes.

Lucky Number: Numerological calculations for your breed reveal your lucky number to be 3.

Notable Italian Greyhound People: Catherine Bell, Frederick the Great of Prussia, Mary Stuart, Sigourney Weaver

Personality and Character: Maltese people ooze success, and you strive for perfection in everything you do. You are competent, thorough, logical, and trusting. You can always be relied on to say just the right thing, for example. In business, you can survive anything by being stubbornly assertive and sticking with something until it is done. You like to try things out with your own hands. However, in some cases, your powerful self-image is based on your accomplishments, which indeed are many, rather than upon your fine character. If you feel that "achievements" are lacking, you are susceptible to dark moods and insecurities. This is a faulty self-assessment but perhaps to be expected, considering how high your standards are. (You tend to cultivate your feelings in private, however, so no one else may be aware of them.) In a social situation, you are the center of attention, and you are always on the go. You like to treat yourself well, yet you place the needs of others above yourself. You are extremely sensitive and creative, especially when it comes to charming others into what needs to be done. Perhaps you are a bit too much of a status seeker, and you have been accused of being a hypocrite, however unfairly.

Best Trait: Your charm is your best trait.

Your Space: The most important room in your house is the living room, and yours is a showplace. It is actually rather theatrical and expresses your imagination. You like abstract area rugs, theatrical lighting, fluid lines, and watercolors, especially mauve and purple. Many Maltese people also enjoy decorating with aquariums. You are the perfect host and throw the best parties around.

Career: You would excel in the fields of technology and banking, but you need to be at the center of things—the center of power.

Leisure Time and Entertainment: You are interested in sports and also do well at them. One of your favorite artists is the British classicist painter Arthur Wardle—you love his painting of the two Maltese on paper. There is nothing you enjoy more than a sensuous bubble bath. You're also very musical—think about taking up a less-popular instrument, such as the harp.

When it comes to vacation, go for a change of pace and take a trip to Europe, including, of course, Malta.

Fashion Musts: You look best in soft, lightweight materials. Structured jackets paired with a great pair of jeans are your trademark. Unusual and expensive jewelry (especially watches) are your best accessories, and purple and gray are your best colors. Maltese people like exquisitely tailored clothing, like that designed by Teri Jon.

Food Faves: You enjoy delicacies like broiled salmon, sausages, mangoes, and almonds. And malteds, of course. (You crave deliciously scented sweets.)

Significant Others: You have lots of positive energy and are very appealing to others; however, it is difficult to tie you down, and sometimes you have a hard time adjusting to home and family life. (You are really something of a jet-setter.) You need a partner as independent and adventurous as you are.

Other Compatible Breed Personalities: Besides Maltese, you are compatible with Border Collies and Whippets.

Pet Peeve: You don't like getting older.

Lucky Number: Numerological calculations for your breed reveal your lucky number to be 3.

Notable Maltese People: Tony Bennett, Halle Berry, Liberace, Heather Locklear, Elizabeth Taylor

Personality and Character: You social butterfly, you! You are definitely into fads and socializing. You are happy, graceful, witty, and charming. You are also tremendously persuasive—no one can deny that. You try to stand firmly by your principles and are even something of a rebel: You don't in the least mind breaking the "rules" if they get in the way of what you consider important. Your main drawback seems to be an inability to stick to the strict facts, and you sometimes put your own needs before those of others. You are also individualistic and have a well-developed value system—but it's definitely your own. You don't like to change your mind about things, even when the facts are against you. You are thorough and detail-oriented. And although you are a mastermind at small details, you may lack an overall "vision."

Best Trait: Your best trait is your social ability—no one can resist your charms!

Your Space: You like to move around; in fact, you are in constant motion. A home with a sunny garden and plenty of bright flowers is a must. Consider planting a butterfly garden (of course!) with a *Buddleia* (butterfly bush) to anchor it.

Career: If you can't be royalty, try work as a detective or police officer—your eye for detail makes you a good candidate for a multitude of law enforcement careers. Just remember to use your powers for good!

Leisure Time and Entertainment: You are agile and light of foot, so sports come naturally to

you. Nothing gives you greater pleasure than going to parties; in fact, you'd rather go to them than give them. On New Year's Eve, you've been known to pack in seven or eight of them as you flit from one house to another. One of your favorite films is *Papillon*, starring Steve McQueen and Dustin Hoffman—and of course the book of the same name by Henri Charrière. You also like the painting *Papillon With a Ball*, which features your beloved breed, by Malcolm S. Tucker.

When it comes to vacation, summertime trips to Europe are always appreciated. However, what you really like is adventure. Although you intensely dislike cold and rain, you'll put up with a lot for the sake of living a full life. You have a spirit of adventure—you'd like swimming in shark-infested waters or exploring Amazonian jungles—and you fear nothing.

Fashion Musts: You can wear anything, and you know it—so accentuate your beautiful hair and face. You show off to your best advantage in brilliant colors, although it's best to keep the fabric plain and simple (and no elastic waistbands, please). For jewelry, fun, chunky bracelets and necklaces are a must. For your endless nights-about-town, try a funky party dress by Betsey Johnson.

Food Faves: Milkshakes, sausage, and fried potatoes are random favorites. You are also a connoisseur of good bread.

Significant Others: You like everyone but have a preference for handsome strangers who can match you in energy and adventurousness. While you are sometimes afraid to enter emotional relationships, when you do, you are idealistic and passionate. Stay away from those practical types—it just won't work.

Other Compatible Breed Personalities: Besides Papillons, you are compatible with Petits Bassets Griffons Vendéens and Skye Terriers.

Pet Peeve: You dislike it when people let their property get run down.

Lucky Number: Numerological calculations for your breed reveal your lucky number to be 5.

Notable Papillon People: Christina Aguilera, Marie Antoinette, King Henry III of England, George Takei

Pretty and Polished

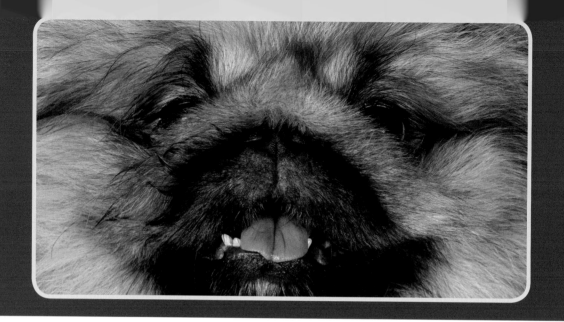

Personality and Character: You are basically a straightforward, uncomplicated person—but one to be reckoned with. You are extremely purposeful, and your number-one goal in life is to be successful. You are very comfortable in a world of competition, and you have a thirst for adventure. You work with sincerity and zeal and are very observant—you don't miss much. You follow through with projects and are good at planning and organizing. And you always find a way to get out of trouble—it's amazing! You're constantly striving to achieve your goals and are never happy until you do, although sometimes your conservative nature may block your path to true success. The word "perfectionist" was made for you. You are cool, dignified, regal, and calm—never one to compromise. You are also not one for being carried away into some fantasy world. You never forget a wrong done to you. Some people feel that you are too critical, and others accuse you of lacking in imagination—two things you strive to improve.

Best Trait: Your sense of purposefulness is your best trait.

Your Space: You enjoy spending time in museums, art galleries, and the like. Many consider your home to be a showplace.

Career: You can start out in food preparation and service, but you won't quit until you own the restaurant. You would also stand out as a police detective, banker, politician, or salesperson. You do best in active, fast-paced jobs.

Your Inner Dog

Leisure Time and Entertainment: You are a tremendously avid reader and enjoy all the classics. In the winter, you love skiing and tobogganing. In the summer, you enjoy gardening and softball. You also have a keen interest in the arts and design.

As far as vacation is concerned, nothing would pique your interest like a trip to the Old Country—in this case China, perhaps to the Forbidden City, which has always held a secret fascination for you.

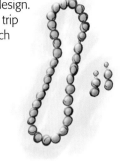

Fashion Musts: You Peke people are elegant. You are extremely careful of your appearance and choose simple, well-tailored, neat, conservative pieces that suit you to a tee. Your best colors are gold, yellow, and dark blue, even though you have a tendency to wear black. Amber and onyx are your perfect jewelry accessories. You have a fondness for Liz Claiborne's classic knitwear designs.

Food Faves: You enjoy chicken salad with bacon, lettuce, and tomato. For dinner, Peking duck, of course. And you'll drink champagne with anything but breakfast, when you must have your espresso.

Significant Others: You have a strong need to give and receive love. Peke people may find it difficult to connect with someone who can meet their expectations. You seek appreciation from your significant other, and you are rather prone to May–December romances. Look for a partner who is neat and orderly around the house.

Other Compatible Breed Personalities: Besides Pekingese, you are compatible with Afghan Hounds and Chihuahuas.

Pet Peeve: You don't like people who live in a fantasy world—and you hate messes.

Lucky Number: Numerological calculations for your breed reveal your lucky number to be 3.

Notable Pekingese People: Barbara Cartland, Joan Rivers, Shirley Temple, Betty White

Pomeranian People

Personality and Character: You value friendship and are one of the most loyal friends someone could have. You have great intelligence, a strong sense of duty toward others, and are capable of very deep love. You are also immensely practical and loaded with common sense and lots of facts, which you can quote ad infinitum. You don't like to take a gamble and are driven by a strong need for security and routine. You are detached, straightforward, and analytical, perhaps too much so. You enjoy a debate, but you can be too critical in your speeches. Some of this is because you are painfully shy, although it may seem to others that you are an extrovert. You are honest and conscientious: People respect you for knowing what the right thing to do is and sticking to it. And you have the strong will to go with it.

Best Trait: You are extremely loyal.

Your Space: Your favorite room is the kitchen, where you can indulge both your practical and creative gifts. It is the centerpiece of your home.

Career: Your deep sense of responsibility and love of knowledge mean that you would make a great teacher or judge.

Leisure Time and Entertainment: You like reading the works of François Rabelais, whose wit and humor strike a deep but subtle chord within you. You enjoy southern rock like the Allman Brothers Band. Pomeranian owners make outstanding chess players, but you also enjoy a good game of football.

When it comes to vacation, go to the Berkshires or China. You love hunting for antiques, and there are few better places to find them. You also might enjoy a trip to Germany—back to the original Pomerania.

Fashion Musts: You look best in houndstooth or herringbone weaves, in light colors, with simple jewelry. For a change of pace, wear red—it will bring out a different side of you. You like classic Hugo Boss designs. (You've considered wearing pom-poms in honor of your dog's breed, but what would people think?!)

Food Faves: You have a definite liking for sweets, especially strawberry shortcake. You are also one of the few people around who really like fruitcake, as long as it is full of raisins and nuts and glacé cherries.

Significant Others: Look for an active, independent, and imaginative partner—you'll make beautiful music together. (Pomeranian people of both sexes are very passionate.)

Other Compatible Breed Personalities: Besides Pomeranians, you are compatible with Cairn Terriers and Fox Terriers.

Pet Peeve: You dislike surprises.

Lucky Number: Numerological calculations for your breed reveal your lucky number to be 7.

Notable Pomeranian People: Fran Drescher, Sharon Osbourne, Elvis Presley, Nicole Richie, LeAnn Rimes

Personality and Character: While Pug people enjoy life, some of you spend too much time as an observer, at least in some respects. Get out more to mix with people! Perhaps you still harbor a subconscious fear of others' reactions to you. On the whole, you are even-tempered. You stay cool even when everyone else is going wild with panic, and even when something goes wrong, you are not discouraged. Most charming of all, you often say some delightful things that people are just not expecting—and they love you for it. In fact, you love to surprise people in small ways. You are impossible to pigeonhole, and that's just the way you like it. You are an idealist, and you tend to be more interested in a general concept than in the details of making it happen. While you do have some good long-term ideas about finances, don't neglect professional advice—to do so might be very costly in the end. You are a great listener.

Best Trait: You're able to keep a cool head no matter what's going on around you.

Your Space: You love your kitchen, but you keep it traditional—but not stale. You can always surprise with your imaginative use of color and fabric. Every room in your house is inviting and warm.

Career: You shine in a career that calls forth your skills in people management. Look for work in human resources.

Leisure Time and Entertainment: You enjoy John Wayne movies, word games, and crossword puzzles. You love candles and bubble baths and listening to jazz musicians like Miles Davis. You also like to catch up on your reading.

For vacation, consider exploring the picturesque charm of San Francisco or the grander beauties of an Alaskan cruise. You'd like to see those glaciers before they melt!

Fashion Musts: You have a great sense of style—show it off! Burgundy and black are good colors for you. There is nothing frumpy in your closet—in fact, most of your clothes are refined and modern. You love designers like Stella McCartney—her mix of the feminine with an unexpected accent detail keeps people guessing. Your best gem is the subtle and sophisticated topaz.

Food Faves: You tend to overindulge with a big breakfast. You also like to have dessert before you eat your meals. And you do like your meals. All of them.

Significant Others: You are tender, loving, and romantic, but your tendency to mistrust can sow seeds of dangerous jealousy. You tend to be shy but are very attractive to those who prefer a sweet rather than spicy personality. However, your emotions are deep and strong. You call it protectiveness, perhaps. A big danger for you is falling in love with someone at work, which may not be a good idea.

Other Compatible Breed Personalities: Besides Pugs, you are compatible with Bernese Mountain Dogs and Scottish Terriers.

Pet Peeve: You hate worrying about details.

Lucky Number: Numerological calculations for your breed reveal your lucky number to be 8.

Notable Pug People: Ted Danson, George Eliot, Billy Joel, Mickey Rourke, Tori Spelling

Pretty and Polished

Personality and Character: You are good-natured, reflective, introspective, and cautious, trusting reason over feelings. You always plan your actions in advance. Although you are outwardly social, you tend to avoid any depth of emotional commitment, and you can be reserved and distant in communications. Sometimes you give credit to other people when you should claim it for yourself. You can be gullible and sometimes lack common sense; however, you have a lot of abilities, which you often underestimate. You tend to work "behind the scenes." You can always be depended on to follow through, but you need a leader you can trust. You are a "doer" and want immediate results. You are gifted with natural, witty eloquence, and you are not shy about complaining when something goes wrong. You place a high value on friendship and are motivated by a sense of loyalty. Your friendships are always long-term, maybe because you believe that everyone is good at heart.

Best Traits: You are inspiring and idealistic.

Your Space: Your living room is your showpiece, filled with Victorian furniture and hand-carved solid wood. Despite all appearances, however, you're really not "into" material possessions. They just sort of accumulate.

Career: You would enjoy a career in finance, science, something in the aircraft industry, or perhaps maintenance. You are not interested in a job that puts you in the spotlight. You'd prefer to let your dog shine for you.

Leisure Time and Entertainment: You love the smooth, romantic sound of fellow Shih Tzu owner Frank Sinatra. When it comes to literature, you enjoy reading detective and crime novels—something where you can put your mind to work but not be bogged down in it. You also like puzzles and games.

Shih Tzu people enjoy going on cruises and other planned vacations that take the worry out of things. You also enjoy the company of other people. You are not one for hiking around in the wilderness!

Fashion Musts: Select fabrics that don't require a lot of care. Yellow and red are your best colors, and they look good on your dog, too. Tommy Hilfiger sportswear would be a good choice for your everyday wear. You don't need a lot of makeup to look your best.

Food Faves: You like grilled steak fajitas and anything fried. You also like sushi, and you can't do without your daily banana. One of your favorite desserts is zeppole. (Sinatra loved it, after all.)

Significant Others: You are a romantic but are sometimes reluctant to show tenderness when you feel it. You tend to be possessive. Your best partner is someone who is both strong-willed and supportive of you. Stay away from anyone who is really competitive.

Other Compatible Breed Personalities: Besides Shih Tzu, you are compatible with Basenjis and Bulldogs.

Pet Peeve: You don't like weddings.

Lucky Number: Numerological calculations for your breed reveal your lucky number to be 3.

Notable Shih Tzu People: Lara Flynn Boyle, Mariah Carey, Nicole Richie, Jane Seymour, Frank Sinatra

Personality and Character: Let's face it, you are strikingly beautiful. Some people consider you frivolous, haughty, self-important, and even a little yappy. That's their problem. You are just a spirited free-thinker and know your own value. You love being pampered. (And no matter what people say, the fact is that you are tremendously popular and get invited to the best parties, which is more than they can say for themselves.) Despite your delicate appearance, you are extremely competitive and don't mind mixing it up with the big guys, sometimes, it is admitted, to your detriment. You can be overly suspicious, and it takes a while for you to warm up to strangers, but you are loyal to the ones you love. (This may not include children, who tend to grab all the attention for themselves.)

Best Traits: Your best traits are your self-possession and assurance.

Your Space: You create a vibrant, exciting environment, even in the smallest places. You are extremely attuned to your surroundings. While you are fond of antiques and silks, you also insist upon a family-friendly kitchen and dining room.

Career: Anything textile—Yorkie people make superior weavers, for instance. If that is too humdrum, the fashion industry awaits, including fashion photography. More than one Yorkie person has also made it big on the tightrope circle.

Leisure Time and Entertainment: Lots of cuddling and some frisky play are always in order. However, the kind of play that you're interested in can be accomplished indoors. You have a take-it-or-leave-it attitude toward nature, mostly leave it. It collides with your hair. You also love to dance, particularly the waltz. In a more adventurous mood, you can count on Yorkie people to take up skydiving.

You enjoy warm, sunny places, like Florida and the Caribbean. Yorkshire, England, might also be worth exploring.

Fashion Musts: Your hair is wonderful! Wear it long to show off that gloss and texture. Your biggest worry is split ends—use a good shampoo to combat them. Yorkie people look best in steel blue with tan or gold accents. You can go with innovative fashion like Dolce & Gabbana, but you also handle a business suit perfectly as well. The metallic look is definitely for you. You love paisley, but only in private. Your jewelry too must be gold—nothing less will do. Citrines look wonderful on you.

Food Faves: Yorkshire pudding and roast beef are favorites. Although Yorkshire is noted for its rare varieties of rhubarb, you don't eat much of that.

Significant Others: Your best friends are usually of the opposite sex—and you enjoy close relationships with people considerably younger or older than yourself. You also enjoy the company of people from a wide variety of social backgrounds. In fact, you tend not to get along with people who are too similar to yourself. You are extremely considerate and tend to give your all in any relationship.

Other Compatible Breed Personalities: Besides the Yorkshire Terrier, you are compatible with Greyhounds and Labrador Retrievers. You have a rather sneaking affection for Clydesdale horses, too.

Pet Peeve: You don't like people disturbing you while you're trying to rest.

Lucky Number: Numerological calculations for your breed reveal your lucky number to be 5.

Notable Yorkshire Terrier People: Audrey Hepburn, Richard Nixon, Joan Rivers, Justin Timberlake, Vanessa Williams

Chapter 2

Fit and Fun

Basenji People • Brittany People • Dachshund People • Flat-Coated Retriever People • German Shorthaired Pointer People • Golden Retriever People • Greyhound People • Labrador Retriever People • Miniature Pinscher People • Miniature Schnauzer People • Pembroke Welsh Corgi People • Portuguese Water Dog People • Scottish Terrier People • Skye Terrier People • West Highland White Terrier People

Basenji People

Personality and Character: You are intelligent, distinguished, and independent, a person who is driven to lead. You are a guider and shaper, a creative leader who makes decisions rationally. You have immense powers of concentration and are interested in knowing exactly how things work. Dedicated and hardworking, you will work all night if that's what it takes to get something done. Generally, you are regarded as benign and good natured, but there is a darker, even wild, side to you. You can be overly suspicious and standoffish, and it takes a while for you to warm up to strangers—yet you dislike being alone. As a boss, you can be a little harsh and demanding, and you are not known for considering the feelings of those around you, although this is a trait that improves with age. You also love being the center of attention and have been known to manipulate the feelings of others. You can be prone to great exaggeration and sometimes like to argue just for the sake of it. You never hold a grudge, though, and you possess an unexpected sense of humor (although your chortling laugh can be a bit unnerving until people get to know you better). Just as an aside, Basenji owners often have elegant handwriting.

Best Trait: You are able to make things happen.

Your Space: The bedroom, the ballroom, and the boardroom are all equally your domain. You are wonderful at incorporating your true self into your home design—every room really reflects you. You like exotic, expensive fabrics and leather and sturdy heirloom furniture. You favor classic, quiet colors such as pale gray for the walls. Your favorite artist is Van Gogh; his brilliant, even exaggerated use of color provides the perfect accent for your quiet walls. You are also a neatnik

Your Inner Dog

as far as your home goes, obsessively clean and particular about every facet of your space. You like your backyard as simple and uncluttered as your home: no lawn ornaments and no prissy flowerbeds, just elegant sculptured shrubs and evergreens.

Career: Basenji owners are made for being in business for themselves, possibly in international import/export or business supplies. You might also enjoy working in a field that helps developing countries get solid economic footing.

Leisure Time and Entertainment: You love NASCAR (something absolutely no one would ever guess). In fact your range of interests is vast. You enjoy dancing (especially ballet), tennis, motorcycles, climbing, chess, and gardening. You even get a great deal of pleasure from ordinary activities such as going to the mall and watching television. You're not much of a reader, but you do subscribe to a lot of magazines—you may need to cut down. You only end up throwing them away, anyway.

Fashion Musts: You like accessories that make a statement, like a long beaded necklace or wide belt. Carry a clutch purse for added chic. Black pants are a staple of your wardrobe, and unlike other people, you never seem to collect dog hair on them. One of your favorite labels is Trussardi—you love its vintage accessories.

Food Faves: You love variety in life, so you enjoy lots of different foods, from basics like beef stew to more gourmet meals like lemon ginger shrimp. You're also a big fan of chocolate trifle—you have quite an affinity for sugar.

Significant Others: You are happiest when paired with someone who is financially secure and educated, someone who takes as much pleasure from life as you do. If you hook up with a softie, you'll walk all over that person and eventually leave the relationship. As for you, the older you get, the sexier you get.

Other Compatible Breed Personalities: Besides the Basenji, you are compatible with Bulldogs and Shih Tzu.

Pet Peeve: You hate flatterers. You can never trust what they are saying.

Lucky Number: Numerological calculations for your breed reveal your lucky number to be 6.

Notable Basenji People: Kelsey Grammer, Queen Juliana of the Netherlands, Courtney Thorne-Smith

Brittany People

Personality and Character: Popular and gregarious, you excel as a member of a group. You are especially good at organizing activities that involve other people, although you sometimes have trouble making plans for yourself. You can get people to do what you want without nagging them, and that's a rare gift. However, you can sometimes overwhelm others with your intensity. You are kind and generous, however, and treat all people equally, whether you like them or not. When people pay you compliments, you tend to change the subject. You are very aware of all the good things that have happened to you, and you never take any of them for granted. You always look on the bright side and know that your life has a strong purpose. You say thank you even for small favors, just one of the many reasons why people like you so much!

Best Trait: You are never too busy to do a favor for someone.

Your Space: You may not be the neatest person around, but you love the way your home looks—besides, a little clutter never hurt anybody. Your favorite room is the family room, where everyone can jumble up together, play games, and have fun. Whatever your home arrangements, you generally fall asleep with your dog lying across your legs. You wake up with a bit of a cramp, but the closeness is worth it.

Career: You need a job where you can work closely with people; in fact, you would be great in caring fields such as sports therapy and teaching physical education. You best job will get you outside, at least sometimes, and in the company of others. Careers that keep you behind a desk all day may not be the best match.

Leisure Time and Entertainment: You try to avoid activities that are physically dangerous, preferring instead to engage in regular exercise with your dog. You have never seen a sport you didn't like but prefer working with a team rather than solitary running. (You don't count jogging with your Brittany as solitary, though—you have the best companion in the world at your heels.) You enjoy playing everything from touch football to basketball—in fact, you have a sport for every season. When indoors, you enjoy computer and console games; you love playing with friends from all around the world.

For vacation, you might enjoy traveling to the French province of Brittany, in honor of your dog. The rugged coastline, the culture, the history—you'll love it. You might also consider a sporty cruise to just about anywhere—you'll meet lots of new friends.

Fashion Musts: When you're hanging out at home or exercising with your dog (and Brittanys need a lot of exercise!), sweats and sneakers are your outfit of choice. You still like to look fashionable, though, and tend to choose more stylish sweat suits, like Juicy Couture. Above all, you like to be comfortable.

Food Faves: You're interested in sampling the traditional foods of Brittany, including galettes and crepes, whiting with braised cabbage, mussels with apple and shallot sauce, and escargot in garlic. And of course, you know your baguettes. When it comes to beverages, you're fond of chouchen, a classic alcoholic beverage of Brittany that is made of fermented honey and water. You also enjoy eating off your best china every day—if you aren't good to yourself, who will be?

Significant Others: Sometimes you make poor choices in relationships. You tend to go for strong-willed types who can't communicate very well. Instead, look for mellow, caring types who can open their hearts.

Other Compatible Breed Personalities: Besides the Brittany, you are compatible with Salukis and West Highland White Terriers.

Pet Peeve: You hate it when people take things for granted.

Lucky Number: Numerological calculations for your breed reveal your lucky number to be 1.

Notable Brittany People: Susan Dey

Dachshund People

Personality and Character: Once self-motivated Dachshund people set their mind to something, it will be accomplished. You are incredibly persistent and focused and may even be accused of badgering people. You can also be a little sharp with others, even when you don't mean to be. On the other hand, you are immensely entertaining, clever, fun-loving, and people-oriented. You are known for your high spirits and your immense faith in yourself. In a few cases, this brashness of temperament can hide some major insecurities—but no one will ever know. You are protective of those you love and would sacrifice anything for them. You are also idealistic and altruistic, but you can easily fall prey to jealousy. You have a lot of love and compassion for others. Emotionally, you are rather impressionable—and patience is not your strong point!

Best Trait: Your unique mix of toughness and tenderness is your best trait.

Your Space: You feel comfortable in the smallest apartment (indeed, claustrophobia is not one of your failings!) and the largest farm or country estate.

Career: Like their doggy counterparts, some Dachshund owners like to work underground. Some are miners, while others turn to spelunking as a hobby. Other Dachshund people excel as writers, artists, inventors, and educators. Whatever you choose, you need a job that gives you independence.

Leisure Time and Entertainment: Your love reading books about the Dachshund; try *Picasso*

& Lump: A Dachshund's Odyssey, by David Douglas Duncan; *Redstripe and Other Dachshund Tales*, by Jack Magestro; *Pretzel*, by H.A. Rey; and anything by P.G. Wodehouse, the famous humorist and Dachshund lover. You also have a secret admiration for Ernest Hemingway—for no particular reason. Your favorite artists are Picasso, El Greco, and Andy Warhol—the wild humor of their work reminds you of your dog.

For vacation, an Alaskan wilderness excursion is right up your alley. Or be adventurous in foreign lands and try Belize or Australia.

Fashion Musts: Dachshund people are especially difficult to pin down when it comes to a representative fashion look—although they are always distinctive and recognizable. You can wear any color, although you look best in blues and greens. It's no coincidence that these were the main colors Waldi, the official mascot (and a wirehaired Dachshund), wore for the 1972 Summer Olympic Games at Munich. You always like a little reminder of that glorious moment. You love designers like Bill Blass who make functional, quality clothing. No matter where you go or what you wear, you're always bombarded by those "Omigosh, you look GREAT!" comments . . . and you love 'em.

Food Faves: Hotdogs and sausages—hopefully not at the same meal. When you go out, you prefer places that are unpretentious and inexpensive.

Significant Others: You tend to idealize others and may suffer disappointment on this account. It's hard to find that special someone who appreciates your best qualities, and Dachshund people frequently have more than one marriage or partnership. You won't stand to be overshadowed, that's for certain. Once you find that perfect partner, however, it's forever. And you always manage to keep in touch with your exes.

Other Compatible Breed Personalities: Besides the Dachshund, you are compatible with Dalmatians and Portuguese Water Dogs.

Pet Peeve: You don't like it when people fixate on money.

Lucky Number: Numerological calculations for your breed reveal your lucky number to be 3.

Notable Dachshund People: James Dean, Carol Lombard, Christian Slater, John Wayne, E.B. White, P.G. Wodehouse

Flat-Coated Retriever People

Personality and Character: You are determined, animated, confident, outgoing, and loving. Even when you are by yourself, you are never bored and can always find something interesting to do. You smile easily and often and are just about one of the nicest people around—everybody likes you and enjoys your almost perpetual good humor! You know the things that really matter in life, and you will stick up for yourself and others, even when you are afraid. You have a deep but private sense of compassion and have been a secret benefactor to more than one person. All the same, there is a mystery about you—others find it impossible to tell what you are really thinking. One failing you have is your short attention span—you need to listen a little more carefully to others. It's amazing what kind of interesting gossip one can pick up just by listening!

Best Trait: Your best trait is your unfailing good humor.

Your Space: You prefer a cozy and intimate space all to yourself where you can read, write, and think. You love your overstuffed chair, for instance. You like low ceilings, natural light, neutral-colored walls, and piled carpeting. You have pillows, plants, pottery, and perhaps a still life. Once you find your ideal decor, it stays there—you are not one for moving furniture around all the time.

Career: You're a good fit in professions like nursing, law, communications (writing or publishing), or the military—you just enjoy being around people. Those of you who have served in the military have done so with uncommon courage, and you bear the scars of it.

Leisure Time and Entertainment: You can come up with fun new things to do all the time, but some of your favorites include poker, bicycling, football, and embroidery. You enjoy walking, even in winter, your favorite season. You especially love walking on the beach with your dog. You read history, as well as Darwin, Marx, and Freud. You especially enjoy British and Canadian authors. You like singing, too, although your voice is frankly—well—don't give up your day job.

When it comes to vacation, you shine in a watery environment, just like your dog. Any place with a beach is fine, but you prefer the tropics.

Fashion Musts: Flat-Coated people look great in vibrant hues, especially red. You have great shoulders and like to emphasize them. You shine in dramatic shawls, asymmetric dresses, and even tailored tweed suits. For those really adventurous moments, a red cape would be dazzling and so you. Norma Kamali is one of your favorite designers—you love her interesting, innovative creations.

Food Faves: Just as you love all kinds of people and activities, your culinary appetite is unbounded as well. You like to experiment, and exotic seafood dishes are a special temptation. You also love chicken and all sorts of fruits and vegetables.

Significant Others: Your serene, happy, optimistic disposition and unfailing presence of mind make you attractive to everyone. You are a passionate lover and a wonderful parent. You strive for a civilized relationship with everyone (including your siblings). In a romantic relationship, you do best with someone who is exceptionally reliable and compassionate—rather like yourself. However, even if you meet up with the wrong sort of person, you are so forgiving that you can generally make everything all right.

Other Compatible Breed Personalities: Besides the Flat-Coated Retriever, you are compatible with Doberman Pinschers and German Shepherd Dogs.

Pet Peeve: You don't like it when people don't bother to shave.

Lucky Number: Numerological calculations for your breed reveal your lucky number to be 9.

Notable Flat-Coated People: Stanley Coren, Lord Tweedmouth of Scotland

German Shorthaired Pointer People

Personality and Character: You are a friendly sort who mixes well with any group. Friendship is very important to you, and you are extremely likeable, as well as loyal. You have a strong desire for peace and fellowship. You are talkative and highly intelligent—and your talkativeness, by the way, is not idle chatter but interesting and often serious conversation. Whatever else people might say about you, you are never boring! Disciplined at work, your major challenge is to face the responsibilities of leadership. Although a few of you have been known to overestimate your abilities, most German Shorthaired Pointer people can accomplish almost anything if they really want to. You have a lot of dreams, but you are smart enough to understand that your life isn't ruined if they don't take shape the way you had originally envisioned. You are friendly and helpful to those in need and naturally concerned with others. You can be a bit impressionable, but it's one of your more endearing qualities.

Best Trait: You never shy away from handling tough situations.

Your Space: The beach, any beach. You also love to garden and have a special affinity for poppies. Your taste is exquisite, and you dislike ostentation and pretentiousness in architecture. You enjoy fluid, graceful lines, and everything in your home is harmonious and proportionate. At home, you tend to keep the windows open even in chilly weather, much to the displeasure of those living with you.

Your Inner Dog

Career: Consider counseling, art, architecture, or writing—any field in which you can both express yourself and help others. You are very enthusiastic about your work, but you enjoy learning so much that you are a perpetual student as well. (You've never managed to make that class reunion, but then all the really interesting people never go.)

Leisure Time and Entertainment: Your leisure time is as variable as your mood. Sometimes you want to spend the day fishing on the river, while at other times an afternoon spent reading, drawing, or even napping seems ideal. Books are sacred to you (you can't resist a thriller by Ken Follett), but any type of art is your passion. When it comes to music, you like classic rock like the Rolling Stones. And you never miss a Cirque du Soleil production when it comes around.

For vacation, it's New York for the chic in you and Atlantis for your more mystical side. (So there is no such place as Atlantis—but you can always dream.)

Fashion Musts: You are a trendsetter who is unafraid to try new things, including the latest in hats. You look great in bold, unusual prints, but solids suit you, too. (A nice gray will show off your dog well.) You like to pair up the unexpected, like leather with lace or a silk top with jeans. Big, chunky rings and bracelets are good accessories for you. You're a fan of designers who aren't afraid to step out of the box, like Heatherette.

Food Faves: Your favorites include giblet gravy, pearl onions, candied sweet potatoes, and green bean casserole. Anything at all that reminds you of Thanksgiving, your favorite holiday, a time of peace and fellowship.

Significant Others: You are lucky in love, and when you are not in love, you sometimes feel the sting of loneliness. You would do really well to match up with an artist or a musician, especially a drummer.

Other Compatible Breed Personalities: Besides the German Shorthaired Pointer, you are compatible with Cavalier King Charles Spaniels and Italian Greyhounds.

Pet Peeve: You hate movies and books with stupid endings.

Lucky Number: Numerological calculations for your breed reveal your lucky number to be 1.

Notable German Shorthaired People: Christy Turlington

Golden Retriever People

Personality and Character: It's a cliché, but you really are "golden." You are a cheerful, smart, fun-loving person who enjoys the company of other people. A community-minded good citizen, you have a strong need to serve others and help them—you are very practical in this regard. (It is wonderful to see how many friends you have.) Honest, reliable, and trustworthy, you are never quarrelsome or hostile. You like to give of yourself and never expect a reward. Also, your peacefulness and dependability are legend. However, when disappointed in others, you find it hard to forgive. You also need to stop worrying about the past so much—let it go!

Best Trait: You have the ability to inspire others.

Your Space: Your couch—curled up watching an old movie. You prefer home decor that features matching or at least complementary colors, like dark greens, creams, and browns. You enjoy simplicity and natural materials like stone and oak flooring. Your home is always clean and tidy. If you have a garden, try growing vegetables—Golden Retriever people often find that they have a green thumb.

Career: Golden Retriever people often excel at almost anything—from accounting to zoology. Because you are so reliable and trustworthy, you may have a career in securities and commodities. You have also thought of opening up a little bed and breakfast—it's a lot of work, but it would appeal to your nurturing instincts.

Your Inner Dog

Leisure Time and Entertainment: You love baseball and other traditional sports, like football and soccer. You also like clocks, crafts, gardening, and kitchen gadgets. And nothing can keep you away from shopping at the outlets—you were made for it.

For vacation, there's nothing you like more than spending time with your family. Consider taking a trip to Disney World or eco-tours to family-friendly Costa Rica.

Fashion Musts: Tailored, form-fitting cuts suit you well, especially knits. But your favorite is that old, old sweater. You are just as attached to your old clothes as you are to your loved ones—and that is a strong attachment. Despite your rather dressed-down appearance at times, you like to jazz it up with a great pair of shoes or a fun accessory, like a belt. Greens and golds are flattering colors for you. You like designers who make simple, comfortable clothes, like Eileen Fisher.

Food Faves: You have a great weakness for snack items, especially jelly beans, but you try to stay healthy with foods that are organically grown. You are also careful to feed your dog as well as you feed yourself. You also enjoy making your own soups—they are so soothing and nurturing. Chicken noodle is one of your favorites.

Significant Others: You desire partnership. While you get along with everyone, someone who is sincere, open-minded, and respectful has the best chance of winning your heart.

Other Compatible Breed Personalities: Besides the Golden Retriever, you are compatible with Australian Shepherds and Miniature Schnauzers.

Pet Peeve: Bad dates are your biggest pet peeve.

Lucky Number: Numerological calculations for your breed reveal your lucky number to be 6.

Notable Golden Retriever People: Neil Diamond, Mary Tyler Moore, Bill Murray, Paul Newman, Conan O'Brien

Greyhound People

Personality and Character: You are a paradox and a mystery. On one hand, you're sleek and elegant almost to a fault. (Find out if you have noble or even royal blood in your veins—perhaps going back for centuries.) You are quiet, prudent, and reserved, and your loyal nature helps you both attract and retain friends. You also have a gentle disposition that is a joy to all who know you. What you do hide is the easy-to-overlook fact that you have—well—a killer instinct. At work, you are incredibly competitive. You are the natural leader, and anyone who is in your life must understand that. Let's face it: You're always two steps ahead of everyone else. However, you can and do leave it at the office. At home, you're a different animal, so to speak. There you are pleasant, gentle, and quiet, although you do want things just so. You enjoy the company of others and prefer not to be alone.

Best Trait: You have a noble nature.

Your Space: A large yard and comfortable couch are equally important. You are also very fond of your bed. You dislike extremes of temperature and insist on climate control at all times. You are a traditionalist in your choice of furnishings.

Career: Your drive and ambition could certainly help you become an executive at a major corporation. You might also excel in the sports or transportation industries.

Leisure Time and Entertainment: You like to read anything *racy*, really—Harlequin romances are one of your guilty pleasures. You also like books about your breed—try *Dorian Greyhound*, by Sheryl Longin. When it comes to television, you like *The Simpsons*, if only because it features a Greyhound. You also enjoy participating in sports, especially track and field events. A fast car is one of your indulgences—you love the BMW 5 series.

When it comes to vacation, you stay away from both the beach and ski slopes—they're too crowded, too hot, or too cold. England makes a great getaway because it brings to mind the glory days of your dog, when only royalty could own a Greyhound.

Fashion Musts: People think that you spend hours at the gym or track to get that look, but actually it's all right there in the genes. Short hair looks great on you, and you are an expert at applying subtle makeup. Bright colors are especially suitable for you, although people often tell you how good you look in gray. With your wonderful neck, you can get away with a splendid choker—try a strand of pearls. Your height and build convey true elegance, so you should wear clothes that accentuate it. Try the sheath dress—it was made for you. You like chic, elegant designers like Giorgio Armani.

Food Faves: You are quite fond of game meat, such as venison and wild boar, the very items your dog used to hunt.

Significant Others: You get along best with confident and mature people, but you can't help being just a little competitive, even with them. You are generally tolerant of other people's kids, although they do tend to annoy you when they're not well behaved. When it comes to love and relationships, always trust your instincts.

Other Compatible Breed Personalities: Besides the Greyhound, you are compatible with Labrador Retrievers and Yorkshire Terriers.

Pet Peeve: You dislike it when people make a point of telling you what they think, even when you don't care.

Lucky Number: Numerological calculations for your breed reveal your lucky number to be 9.

Notable Greyhound People: Bo Derek, Frederick the Great of Prussia, General George A. Custer

Labrador Retriever People

Personality and Character: No wonder you're popular! You are interested in serving others. You are friendly without being effusive, hardworking with plenty of time to play, and energetic without losing your essential calm. You can be competitive but in such a subtle way that others may not even be aware of it. You are diplomatic, hard-working, and dependable. You are always cheerful, even during tense times—one reason that people like having you around. You love children of all ages; in fact, you love everybody. Labrador people are the opposite of loners, and when deprived of good company for even a brief period, you may go into a "decline." Labrador owners also traditionally give the best parties on the block. You are very intelligent and are a lifelong learner—consider going back to college or working on that advanced degree! Labrador people are also known for their patriotism, adaptability, and incredible charm.

Best Trait: You are extremely dependable.

Your Space: The most important room in the house is the bathroom—and yours must be exactly right for true happiness. You'd prefer a Jacuzzi, of course, but you also like brisk showers and leisurely bubble baths. Your entire home is a reflection of your personality, and you like unusual woods and finishes to express it. You also love your collection of wooden duck decoys—it reminds you of all the duck hunting you and your Lab have done, if only in your dreams.

Career: Labrador people can take on hard physical work but are also wonderful in the healing and helping professions. Consider a career in psychology, chiropractic, or public relations. If that doesn't appeal to you, any outdoor, sporty kind of career might.

Leisure Time and Entertainment: You are good at all outdoor activities, especially swimming, and do best in an environment where you can indulge your passion for this and other sports. A picnic with swimming is your idea of a great afternoon. Labrador people prefer adventure stories without too much violence and romances that aren't overloaded with sex. One of your favorite music groups is the Doors—not in the least because their name brings to mind your favorite breed.

For vacation, choose a place that's cold, wet, and wild, like Newfoundland. Whitewater rafting might also be suitable.

Fashion Musts: Labrador people go for the natural look and do best in earth tones of black, chocolate, and muted gold. Jewelry is unnecessary for you—you are too busy to bother with it. When you wear anything of that nature, turquoise is a good choice. Let your creativity come through in your hairstyle as well. Some of you are into leather. For casual wear (which is as often as possible), boot-cut jeans are a must. You love classic sportswear designers like Calvin Klein.

Food Faves: Labrador people are not usually picky eaters. In fact, you will eat anything and require nothing fancier than beans and franks. And chocolate. As long as you have plenty of it, you'll be happy.

Significant Others: Labrador people often do well with a partner who is sports-minded and full of energy but also easygoing. You cherish your family and friends and are attracted to people who do the same.

Other Compatible Breed Personalities: Besides the Labrador Retriever, you are compatible with Greyhounds and Yorkshire Terriers.

Pet Peeve: You hate it when people fail to see the humor in things.

Lucky Number: Numerological calculations for your breed reveal your lucky number to be 8.

Notable Labrador Retriever People: Dick Cheney, Bill Clinton, Rupert Everett, Brad Garrett, Steve Martin, Gwyneth Paltrow

Miniature Pinscher People

Personality and Character: You have a clear set of principles, and you live by them. You find strength in yourself, although some have accused you of being self-righteous. You are completely self-possessed and are a born leader—you enjoy taking control of a situation. (You have a great eye for detail and think that almost anything can be analyzed.) You also excel at finding practical solutions to real problems. Fearless and spirited, you are definitely willing to go into uncharted waters—you feel at home in an unpredictable and uncontrollable world. In fact, you love challenges and even opposition, and you enjoy overcoming obstacles. You do require lots of good company and have a strong need to be with like-minded friends to whom you are extremely dedicated. You have a silly side, but it becomes apparent only to your best friends. Some Min Pin people are far too attached to their possessions.

Best Trait: Your leadership skills are second to none.

Your Space: The most important space in your house is the deck or patio—that's where you do most of your living anyway, including the cooking. (You are addicted to your grill!) Because the patio is an extension of your home and you like to make sure that it's well appointed, consider adding little touches like teak benches, landscape lighting, a statuary, birdhouses, or sundials.

Career: You are easily bored by dull work or dull people but flourish when allowed to make your own decisions about your work environment and job assignments. Money is not important to you, and you prefer intellectually demanding work in which you carry a lot of responsibility, especially if it benefits other people. Possible careers include publishing, the law, or something in a health-related field, like speech pathology.

Leisure Time and Entertainment: In their leisure time, Min Pin owners gravitate to physical exercise, with lots of sweat involved. You have found that a good workout helps take your mind off of things. You especially enjoy team sports, including water sports like water polo. When it comes to literature, mysteries and nonfiction exposés pique your interest. Your favorite music is that good old standby, European classical. If it was good enough for Bach, it's good enough for you.

For vacation, consider taking a trip into the past—perhaps a childhood haunt that evokes tender memories. Don't go anywhere that you went with your ex, though, no matter how tempting. If you have no fond memories of childhood, grab your current squeeze and make some new tender memories of your own—just the two of you. It doesn't really matter where you go.

Fashion Musts: When it comes to fashion, well-fitted pants are a closet staple for you. Whether trousers for work or capris and denim for everyday, you own them all! For an especially flattering fit, try some pants by label Alice + Olivia, and jazz things up with an interesting shoe in a contrasting color or texture. You also enjoy changing your hair and makeup every few months—variety suits you. (Be careful not to overuse the hair products, though—a little bit goes a long way!)

Food Faves: You enjoy cooking and like to eat anything you can grill, including vegetables, meat, and seafood. The one bad eating habit you have is cutting the crusts off your bread. That's the good part, you know!

Significant Others: You are gentle, caring, romantic, and loving; however, you also may cling to unworthy emotional attachments. Think carefully before getting together with someone at your job, even though it may be tempting. Look for a partner who can be an equal, someone with whom you can explore places and ideas. You need a mate who's as open and honest as you are.

Other Compatible Breed Personalities: Besides the Miniature Pinscher, you are compatible with Boston Terriers and Chow Chows.

Pet Peeve: You're bothered by people who don't keep their promises.

Lucky Number: Numerological calculations for your breed reveal your lucky number to be 4.

Notable Miniature Pinscher People: Joey Fatone, Michellie Jones, Christina Ricci

Miniature Schnauzer People

Personality and Character: You are creative, friendly, and extremely intuitive about other people. In fact, you're the one to call to mediate between hostile parties. You are loaded with common sense and practicality, combined with a good deal of worldly sophistication. You work to complete every task on time. You will also go far out of your way to save a friend who is in trouble. Sometimes you are so eager to put your ideas into action that you can neglect your physical needs. You can also lack in emotional restraint and can be moody, impulsive, or depressed. You also have trouble making a plan and sticking to it. In this way, you can be prone to self-sabotage. Try not to base your self-image on your possessions—rather, focus on the many fine character traits you possess, especially your creativity.

Best Trait: Your creativity is your best trait.

Your Space: Your favorite room is your bedroom. In this private space, you can express your real self: bold, with an eclectic design sense. Your large platform bed with its massive headboard is definitely the focal point of the room. It may be a little wild for some—but then you don't invite many people in there.

Career: You would be excellent in fields that call for an inventive mind, such as arts and crafts, teaching, and writing.

Leisure Time and Entertainment: You enjoy all kinds of sports, and yoga is one of your favorite activities. You are also an art aficionado who is especially drawn to post-Impressionist painters like Henri de Toulouse-Lautrec. You love celebrations of all sorts: birthday parties, weddings, Fourth of July picnics, Labor Day barbecues, Thanksgiving get-togethers, Christmas caroling, New Year's parties, Halloween parties, Just Because It's Today parties—you name it!

When it comes to vacation, you enjoy traveling and have some of your most interesting adventures when you travel alone. Consider exploring the Finger Lakes region—you will appreciate the deep beauty of this area.

Fashion Musts: Take extra care of your eyebrows—invest in a good set of tweezers. You don't want to look too much like your dog. Also, go for dramatic makeup and more than one eclectic accessory—you can get away with it. Bold colors like reds, deep blues, and purples look great on you. Prints, especially geometric patterns, are quite flattering. You love cutting-edge fashion—try a look by avant-garde designer Miguel Adrover.

Food Faves: Spicy Cajun jambalaya is one of your favorites. And of course you like salt and pepper on everything—they remind you of your dog.

Significant Others: Although you are capable of deep affection and self-sacrifice, you can also be emotionally fickle. You require a lot of freedom in a relationship. On account of this, there may be more than one marriage or relationship in your life.

Other Compatible Breed Personalities: Besides the Miniature Schnauzer, you are compatible with Australian Shepherds and Golden Retrievers.

Pet Peeve: You don't like it when cashiers don't pay attention.

Lucky Number: Numerological calculations for your breed reveal your lucky number to be 9.

Notable Miniature Schnauzer People: Bill Cosby, Bob Dole, Bruce Lee, Mary Tyler Moore

Pembroke Welsh Corgi People

Personality and Character: Optimistic, intelligent, loyal, and unique, Pembroke people have a regal air all their own, just like Queen Elizabeth of England, who is the world's most famous Corgi breeder. You have a high sense of justice—in fact, you always take the side of those who are wronged. Indeed, you Pembroke people are known for your gallantry, patriotism, and love of honor. You like to be the center of attention, and you sometimes lack humility. You are also a bit of a gossip, which has gotten you into trouble (more than once).

   Sometimes you have too rigid a commitment to the rules of society. You have high expectations for your family members, although sadly, most of your relatives do not live up to them. It's not really their fault, though. Times have changed, so it would be wise to be less critical. You have great emotional balance.

Best Trait: Your emotional stability is your best trait.

Your Space: As a rule, you dislike cities and prefer to live in the suburbs in a relatively new house. You enjoy remodeling it, enclosing porches, adding extra bedrooms, that sort of thing. You also enjoy entertaining.

Career: You despise mechanical labor but would excel in the health care, science, and philosophical fields.

Leisure Time and Entertainment: You are a great fan of bicycling and

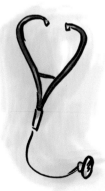

ice skating. We won't talk about all the times you've been seen at wild parties. Classics, like Chaucer, are high on your reading list (or should be). But you have a secret love for Stephen King horror novels, too—after all, he is a fellow Corgi lover. You also have a natural flair for the arts and enjoy collecting beautiful things.

When it comes to vacation, be adventurous and go someplace far away, like India, for a few weeks. You know you love to travel.

Fashion Musts: Physically, your wonderful neck and nice nose are remarkable, so it's nice to show these off by keeping your hair away from your face. You are a fashion guru, and it shows. Bold colors, especially reds, blues, and golds (although not worn simultaneously), are your best. You wear clothes with such fluid grace that you draw attention wherever you go. For an eye-catching look, try a vintage Dior hat.

Food Faves: Your favorite foods include quiche; try Queen Elizabeth's favorite recipe, quiche with onions, artichokes, asparagus, and tomatoes. When you're not being so regal, you like curly fries.

Significant Others: Pembroke people can be demanding of their mates, but they are extremely loyal. Don't always trust your instincts when it comes to love—they have led you astray before. Use reasoned judgment as well—you may have more success this way.

Other Compatible Breed Personalities: Besides the Pembroke Welsh Corgi, you are compatible with Neapolitan Mastiffs and Rhodesian Ridgebacks.

Pet Peeve: You hate it when things don't work properly.

Lucky Number: Numerological calculations for your breed reveal your lucky number to be 6.

Notable Pembroke Welsh Corgi People:
Kirstie Alley, Ava Gardner, Stephen King, Queen Elizabeth II of England

Portuguese Water Dog People

Personality and Character: Ambitious yet idealistic, the Portuguese Water Dog person dances through life. Your flexibility and balance, both physical and mental, make it pretty easy for you to get through each day. You are someone who can manage to get what you want—a special class at a convenient time, an extra ten percent off a price, you name it. You have tremendous natural warmth, and that comes through in all your interactions with people. You are the one who can intercede with a prickly boss on behalf of others. (You're a lover, not a fighter.) You also love entertaining, and you are so organized that you do it with ease. You are not fond of making snap decisions, and that's a good thing in your case—your first inclination may well be wrong.

Best Traits: Your flexibility and compassion are your best traits.

Your Space: You're happy anywhere there's a party—whether it's a wine and cheese gathering or a Mexican fiesta. Your kitchen is the center of your life, and it's all about tradition—cozy but with plenty of functional space. You also love your office, which you have made into a perfect little retreat. If you have a garden, plant chrysanthemums—they'll brighten your day. An almond tree in your garden would be perfect if you have the right climate for it. It will remind your dog of Portugal.

Career: You would excel in the art and entertainment fields—anything that allows you to express yourself.

Leisure Time and Entertainment: Dancing, dancing, and dancing—with the stars, under the stars, whatever. In your spare time, you enjoy bargain hunting. You also love sports, especially baseball. (When you are under pressure, you participate in sports to relieve the tension.) You like country music, including that by Johnny Cash, as well as reggae and ska. For a romantic evening, of course, nothing beats reading *Sonnets From the Portuguese*.

For vacation, a trip to Portugal might be right up your alley. You'd love to visit your dog's ancestral home. In fact, anywhere on the Iberian Peninsula is ideal.

Fashion Musts: You love your little black dress, but you also look great in denim, corduroy, and cotton t-shirts. You're also pretty fond of hand-knit Norwegian sweaters. You look best in soft rather than harsh, bright colors. Tommy Hilfiger sportswear would be a good choice for your everyday wear.

Food Faves: True to your dog's heritage, you like Portuguese specialties: fresh fish (grilled sardine, horse mackerel) and shellfish. Try the national dish, *bacalhau*, or dried, salted cod. For a nonseafood delight, indulge in the Portuguese *cozido à portuguesa*, a thick stew with vegetables and pork. And like the Portuguese, you have a great fondness for cinnamon and curry powder. Your favorite dessert is *pastéis de nata*, a small custard tart sprinkled with cinnamon. It's really good!

Significant Others: It is important for you to stay open to new possibilities. Don't commit yourself too quickly—many times, Portuguese Water Dog people tend to commit to the first person they fall in love with. When in a relationship, you are completely devoted to your partner. You're also great with children.

Other Compatible Breed Personalities: Besides the Portuguese Water Dog, you are compatible with Dachshunds and Dalmatians.

Pet Peeve: You hate it when people don't give their dogs enough exercise.

Lucky Number: Numerological calculations for your breed reveal your lucky number to be 6.

Notable Portuguese Water Dog People: Carlos Ruiz Camino, Ted Kennedy

Scottish Terrier People

Personality and Character: You may be the most balanced of all dog owners. On the one hand, you are bold, vibrant, and a little jaunty. (You have your own special walk.) You are also very kind and idealistic. Determined, thoughtful, and logical, you have a strong sense of duty and responsibility. Life to you is a serious business, and you need a purpose in all that you do. You have no time for distractions. You can, however, procrastinate, and there is a danger of your getting bogged down in petty little details. You are extremely stubborn but adaptable when convinced that a change is necessary. Indeed, you are excited by new ideas and projects. You are respected by all, although you can be domineering, and you may take offense when misunderstood. You are a true philosopher and are quite capable of enjoying your own company. You are absolutely honorable—but you never forget a slight, either. And you don't like being pressured.

Best Trait: Many people appreciate your sense of honor and idealism.

Your Space: The couch. This is your private space, and you share it with no one other than your dog—when he lets you on it, of course. You are interested in all sorts of furnishings. (You may regard this as a pun on the "furnishings," or long hair and underskirt, of the Scottish terrier, in which case you would be quite right.) On a wider level, no place suits you as well as the White House. After all, between at least two presidents, Scotties have spent many years ruling the roost.

Career: You are loaded with technical skills, so consider a job in math, computer science, or medicine. If you work on your time management skills, you would also excel in a management position.

Leisure Time and Entertainment: You enjoy dancing and have a real talent for instrumental music. Try boxing as exercise—it's a sport as tough as your Scottie. You're also a big reader and especially enjoy the mysteries of S.S. Van Dine, who had a Scottish Terrier.

For vacations, try Scotland! Long walks in the heaths and moors are tonic for your blood. On the other hand, you're not averse to a vacation in sunny Mexico, either.

Fashion Musts: It's easy to think "plaid," but that is what everyone expects from you. You're just not that conventional! You often wear glamorous, somewhat expensive clothing—Christian Lacroix is one of your favorite designers. Your handbag is plain, but you adore accessorizing with jewelry, no matter whether it's precious or costume.

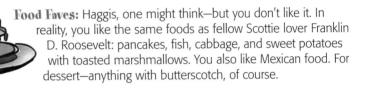

Food Faves: Haggis, one might think—but you don't like it. In reality, you like the same foods as fellow Scottie lover Franklin D. Roosevelt: pancakes, fish, cabbage, and sweet potatoes with toasted marshmallows. You also like Mexican food. For dessert—anything with butterscotch, of course.

Significant Others: You enjoy meeting new people (even if your dog doesn't), and that includes lots of new love affairs! You like to play the field and want to take your time finding the ideal mate. Some Scottish Terrier people are quite demanding of the attentions of others and not very good at giving it back. You have a tendency to get bored in relationships, so you need someone who is going to keep you intrigued. Stay away from stubborn types—you are stubborn enough for any three people. You need to find someone who is a friend as well as a lover.

Other Compatible Breed Personalities: Besides the Scottish Terrier, you are compatible with Bernese Mountain Dogs and Pugs.

Pet Peeve: You hate it when people refuse to learn from past experiences.

Lucky Number: Numerological calculations for your breed reveal your lucky number to be 8.

Notable Scottish Terrier People: Humphrey Bogart, George H.W. Bush, Zsa Zsa Gabor, Franklin D. Roosevelt

Skye Terrier People

Personality and Character: You have a truly beautiful personality: calm, honest, and steadfast. You also have an incredible depth of emotion and feel blessed to wake up every morning. On a social level, you are the life of any party: You're cheerful and chatty, and you love to socialize with groups. While it's right that you should enjoy your very active social life, beware of scandal—you can get yourself into some messes by accidentally saying or doing the wrong thing. You are also generous to the extreme—maybe even too much so. You are dedicated to your work, but you need positive reinforcement to feel good about yourself. You can be the tiniest bit lazy (or at least unambitious) in this regard, but in every other way you are a dynamo.

Best Trait: Your best trait is your unimpeachable ethics.

Your Space: You really love winter, and nothing makes you happier than building a snowman in the front yard. Around the house, there's no place like the living room—as long as it has windows and a skylight to let you enjoy the beautiful views all around you.

Career: Fields where you work with others, such as in sales or as a dental hygienist, artist, teacher, or coach, appeal to you. You don't have vast career ambitions—any good job that pays the bills is fine.

Leisure Time and Entertainment: You're a fan of nonimpact sports like archery, and you enjoy outdoor excursions like canoeing and hiking. When it comes to music, you like contemporary pop by artists like Celine Dion and Madonna. For relaxation, you might want to consider taking a watercolor class or a meditation seminar. As a side note, Skye people often like convertibles, open to the sky. (Coincidence?) A car with a sunroof is also a good option.

You are active and adventurous and have a deep-seated love of travel. A weekend in the mountains would make a great getaway. But for real adventure, there is no place like the Isle of Skye itself, with its wild seacoast and craggy mountains.

Fashion Musts: Silver accessories are just perfect for you. Go for a hairstyle that's easy to care for—it's hard enough combing out the dog. For a different look, try a subtle but daring highlight, like a deep purple. The same goes for clothes: Subtly daring should be your watchwords. Try Moschino for a fun, feminine look.

Food Faves: When it comes to foods, it should be mentioned that you are a picky eater—you have to watch your figure, of course. Many Skye people won't go to a restaurant unless they see the menu first. If left to your own devices, you'd eat a lot of party food. For drinks, your favorite is actually sparkling fresh water, but you also love red wine.

Significant Others: Skye people are passionate lovers and very good at attracting romance—with lots of partners. You may tend to fall in and out of love rather quickly. Look for someone with opinions that coincide with your own. Your biggest fault when it comes to relationships is being unrealistic about what to expect. Marriage is not essential for your dignity or happiness, but having a lot of "special friends" is.

Other Compatible Breed Personalities: Besides the Skye Terrier, you are compatible with Papillons and Petits Bassets Griffons Vendéens.

Pet Peeve: You don't like it when people fail to appreciate what they have.

Lucky Number: Numerological calculations for your breed reveal your lucky number to be 9.

Notable Skye Terrier People: Mary, Queen of Scots, Queen Victoria of England

West Highland White Terrier People

Personality and Character: You are a truly dynamic person, bright, self-reliant, and spontaneous. You know how to live life to the fullest, and you get excited about moving ahead—there is a world of possibilities out there. At the same time, you are self-disciplined and have an unusually good eye for detail. You are independent and acutely intelligent—you have a tremendous desire for knowledge. You are willing to work hard today for rewards tomorrow, and you have a strong sense of responsibility. You also care deeply about politics and the environment. No matter what is going on around you, you tend to be both kind and honest—a difficult combination to achieve. On the darker side of your personality, if you are wronged (and you are very proud), you will take revenge. Also, you can be a little argumentative at times, but you are still a lot of fun to be with. Be sure to listen to the advice of those who have proven themselves trustworthy.

Best Trait: Your enthusiastic nature is your best trait.

Your Space: Your favorite room is your bedroom, which you tend to decorate in various shades of white. This not only matches your dog but gives you the open, airy environment you crave. Whenever possible, you keep the windows open to let in the sights and scents of the outdoors.

Career: Information technology, quality assurance analysis, or even film-making are perfect for you—you have just the right mix of an eye for detail and creativity that can make you a success. Your career ambitions can be realized if you are persistent. (You have a tendency to change jobs in a hurry.)

Leisure Time and Entertainment: You like noncontact sports like rollerblading, roller skating, snowboarding, ice skating, and dancing. When it comes to music, you're a fan of the Celtic sound; it's Thistle & Shamrock all the way. You even like bagpipes!

For vacation, consider the Highlands, of course; you love to be alone with nature. But you don't just walk around up there—you're climbing mountains, rafting, pony trekking, and even taking a scuba dive or two to look for Nessie, the Loch Ness monster.

Fashion Musts: You are very conscious of how you look, and style is important to you. You look equally great in neutrals and bold, vibrant colors. (And there's nothing like a kilt, is there?) You also like lots of leather. Whether you're on a date or going out with some friends for a night on the town, cutting-edge silhouettes look fantastic on you—for added drama, try a mini dress by Proenza Schouler. And for an everyday look, don't forget designer and fellow Westie owner Tommy Hilfiger.

Food Faves: Because you like to get up and running early in the morning, a full breakfast with bacon, eggs, sausage, and pancakes is necessary to your well-being. You may skimp on lunch or dinner, but breakfast—never!

Significant Others: You need to be careful when considering a potential romantic liaison—it can get you into trouble. You tend to choose people who may stray unless you give them a great deal of attention. On the other hand, you have no problem spending time alone. It doesn't bother you a bit.

Other Compatible Breed Personalities: Besides the Westie, you are compatible with Brittanys and Salukis.

Pet Peeve: You hate doing laundry.

Lucky Number: Numerological calculations for your breed reveal your lucky number to be 9.

Notable Westie People: Charles Darwin, Tommy Hilfiger, Amanda Holden

Chapter 3
Valiant and Vivacious

American Staffordshire Terrier People • Boxer People • Bulldog People • Bullmastiff People • Chow Chow People • Doberman Pinscher People • Fox Terrier People • German Shepherd Dog People • Great Pyrenees People • Mixed-Breed People • Petit Basset Griffon Vendéen People • Rhodesian Ridgeback People • Rottweiler People • Shar-Pei People • Saint Bernard People

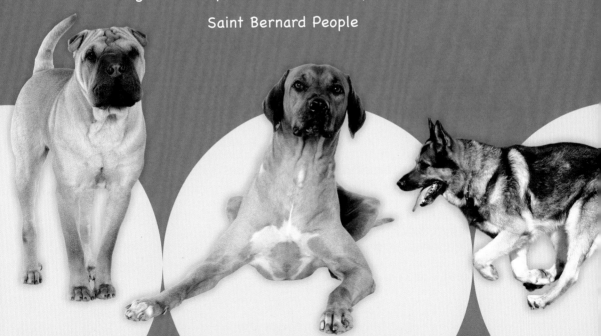

Personality and Character: You are dripping with initiative, but at the same time you are serious and quiet. Intelligent and well informed, you are not afraid of hard work, and you like to keep close tabs on how things are progressing. You love intellectual pursuits but may tend to forget the human factor in the process. Some people think that you have a lack of imagination. You are progressive, health conscious, and interested in a variety of social issues. You are so independent that you may ignore laws if they get between you and what you want done. You think of yourself as a survivor, and on the outside at least, you're as tough as they come, rarely admitting to physical pain or even hurt feelings. Inside, though, you're a softie.

Best Traits: Your independence and initiative are your best traits.

Your Space: Your garden is your haven, and you love growing those Staffordshire flowers: gillyflowers, mints, daisies, primroses, pinks, daffodils, harebells, columbines, sage, lettuce, and parsley. Inside and out, you prefer a logically designed and orderly home. Your garden is full of symmetrical flowerbeds, structured plantings, and neat brick walks. Inside, you have a shelf for everything and prefer light woods with glass accents. You often avoid the kitchen, instead preferring to dine out.

Career: You need to find a career in which you have

independence. Let's face it: You can't stand taking orders. You'd make a great judge, academic scholar, or worker in the humanitarian fields.

Leisure Time and Entertainment: American Staffordshire people enjoy collecting art. (The impressionist Monet is one of your favorites.) You also like reading literary critics Proust and Mallarmé, and you love Greek tragedies (especially Euripides) and great conversations. You train hard for athletic events and often excel at them—rock climbing is one of your favorites. You love fishing, too, and have read Izaac Walton's *Compleat Angler* many times. (Walton was from Stafford, England, as you know.)

For vacation, consider visiting Staffordshire, the ancestral home of your dog. Or for a more fast-paced trip, take a tour of London.

Fashion Musts: Even though fashion is not the most important thing on your mind, you still always manage to look effortlessly put together. You like elegant clothing, and look fabulous in traditional suits and pantsuits with raw silk shirts. For a tailored look, try a suit by designer Giorgio Armani. Shades of blue and rose are particularly flattering on you.

Food Faves: You love sweet desserts, especially ice cream and chocolate candy. On the other hand, for your main meal, you enjoy traditionally British foods that most people consider boring or not particularly tasty, like marmite, toad-in-a-hole, and fish and chips.

Significant Others: You are faithful to your mate, but you sometimes show a lack of imagination in your attentions. For example, you may remember to send flowers and chocolates on important occasions, but they're not the most creative ideas. Read a self-help relationship book to help you spice things up a bit. You love children and are extremely good with them.

Other Compatible Breed Personalities: Besides the American Staffordshire Terrier, you are compatible with Bichons Frises and Collies.

Pet Peeve: Flirts—you are much too serious for that nonsense!

Lucky Number: Numerological calculations for your breed reveal your lucky number to be 9.

Notable AmStaff People: Judd Nelson

Valiant and Vivacious

Boxer People

Personality and Character: You are rebellious, feisty, assertive, fun loving, athletic, and a real individual. You are also organized and always finish what you start. One of the main goals in your life is to be Number One at everything you do, and you usually are. However, beware—your immense energy can overwhelm those people who don't share it. Despite your exuberance, though, you are dependable, sensitive, and kind. You are also incredibly generous with both your time and your money to the less fortunate. The people around you value your great listening skills and the fact that you keep your promises. Acquiring knowledge is very important to you, but you sometimes have trouble applying it for practical purposes. You also have a tendency to make impulsive decisions, and you may make rash statements that you regret later on.

Best Trait: Your exuberance is your best trait.

Your Space: Your den is your favorite room—it's the perfect place for boisterous get-togethers. Your home has cathedral ceilings, skylights, and big picture windows. You are extremely clean, but furniture means little to you. You'd just as soon sleep on a mattress on the floor.

Career: Try the arts or engineering, careers in which you can show off both your exuberant side and your fantastic organizational skills.

Leisure Time and Entertainment: You love sports, especially boxing, of course. You are a superior athlete, talented and tenacious. You're also a fan of art that features your favorite breed, such as the portrait of Ch. Bang Away of Sirrah Crest, now in the American Kennel Club's art collection. A hardcore music fan, some of your favorite groups include classic rock groups the Kinks, the Beatles, and the Rolling Stones. And when it comes to cinema, some of your favorite movies are boxing flicks, like *Rocky*, *Million Dollar Baby*, and *Raging Bull*.

For vacation, try something adventurous, like whitewater rafting down the Colorado or hiking. Action-oriented getaways suit you best.

Fashion Musts: Most Boxer owners look great in light colors. Also, stripes flatter you, unlike most people, so don't be afraid to break out of those boring solid colors! Like Joe Boxer himself, you don't take fashion too seriously—you prefer to have fun. For underwear, well, naturally you wear boxers. And you're more interested in pajamas than party wear. Still, you should indulge in some jewelry—get something as sparkly as you are.

Food Faves: You love sweet things, especially desserts, with key lime and traditional pumpkin pie topping the list. And don't forget the whipped cream! Cauliflower is not one of your favorites—you'll take ice cream instead any day!

Significant Others: You are highly romantic and family minded but are often unluckily drawn to people who are just the opposite. You need to learn that the most fun date is not necessarily the best long-term partner.

Other Compatible Breed Personalities: Besides the Boxer, you are compatible with Siberian Huskies and Weimaraners.

Pet Peeve: You hate it when people interrupt you.

Lucky Number: Numerological calculations for your breed reveal your lucky number to be 1.

Notable Boxer People: Humphrey Bogart, Emily Brontë, Jodie Foster, Shirley MacLaine, Pablo Picasso

Valiant and Vivacious

Bulldog People

Personality and Character: You shun the spotlight and tend to stand back and let other people make the first move. Intelligent and competent, you are completely uninterested in theories or abstractions. You are also very good with money, with a killer instinct for both acquiring it and keeping it. You can make a fortune while other people are losing theirs. What is most wonderful about you is that you really know who you are and what you stand for—which means that you have the opportunity to experience great happiness in your life. You are also quite charming, although you can be extremely private. In fact, although you tend to be cautious, when you do speak you are frank—even blunt—to a fault. People are always a little shocked at this (they're not expecting it), but there you are.

Best Trait: You are extremely self-aware.

Your Space: Comfort is your keynote, and have it you must. Your home is a clever mix of the modern and the nostalgic. You have fabulous taste in decorating, and your home reflects the joys of every season, warm and cozy in the fall, glittering in winter, and sweet and floral in warm weather.

Career: If you are interested in the military, the Marines may make a good fit for you—after all, the Bulldog is their official mascot. Because they are so good with money, Bulldog owners often make successful businesspeople and executives.

Your Inner Dog

Leisure Time and Entertainment: You are a lover of the arts. Your favorite musical artists are the J. Geiles Band, with its raw, muscular sound and swagger, and Santana, whose clever blend of salsa, rock, blues, and jazz appeals to your more eclectic side. You especially love going to concerts and try to get to one once or twice a month. Consider taking up astrology for a hobby—you may have an intuitive gift for it.

For a wonderful vacation, Bar Harbor, Maine, will suit you perfectly. It's quiet, picturesque, and never too hot, so you can take your Bulldog. If you wish to go abroad, try Norway—it's a lot like Bar Harbor.

Fashion Musts: You have a tendency toward dullness in the fashion department, but that is part of your strategy for invisibility. Try adding a small feminine touch to an outfit, like a strand of beads, or choose a skirt with a ruffled hem. For something more feminine, try a Chloé design—the label's signature layered looks could be perfect for you.

Food Faves: You love to eat, and you plan all your meals in advance. You have a real passion for dessert—it's where you show your sweeter side. You particularly love chocolate, apple pie, and crème brûlée. You also like making cakes—and eating them, of course. For the main dish, anything is fine as long as it's not vegetarian.

Significant Others: Bulldog people are seductive and enticing, and they are also amazingly loyal. Still, you generally refuse to take orders—especially from your partner or spouse. You can be deeply hurt if rejected or misunderstood, and you are just the tiniest bit sentimental. You can also be very demanding, in a passive-aggressive sort of way.

Other Compatible Breed Personalities: Besides the Bulldog, you are compatible with Basenjis and Shih Tzu.

Pet Peeve: You hate arguing.

Lucky Number: Numerological calculations for your breed reveal your lucky number to be 1.

Notable Bulldog People: Jessica Biel, Truman Capote, Calvin Coolidge, Warren Harding, Adam Sandler, Reese Witherspoon

Valiant and Vivacious

Bullmastiff People

Personality and Character: Fearless, confident, and reliable, you are a person of great integrity. Courage is your trademark. You are friendly and outwardly focused, with wonderful perseverance and creativity. It is not often that these traits meld so perfectly in one person! Just as the Bullmastiff combines the best qualities of the Bulldog and Mastiff, you have the best qualities of the thinker and the doer. You are also kind, tolerant, and peaceful, although you never hesitate to speak your mind. A realistic person, you are an accurate judge of yourself and your skill levels. You enjoy bringing laughter and smiles to others, and you are known to be fair and a good leader. You also have excellent qualities of self-control, and you are both prudent and humble, especially about your many accomplishments. Your main flaw is that you can be a bit of a slob at times.

Best Trait: Your integrity is your best trait.

Your Space: You love the garden, especially at dawn. Roses are your specialty, and you always have a vase of fresh flowers, for you have a deep love of beauty. As for your house, the bigger the house, the more places you have to throw things. At the very least, a huge front porch is necessary. Your kitchen is all about stainless steel, granite countertops, and a variety of gadgets.

Career: You would do best in a challenging, competitive, entrepreneurial career, and you would work very well on commission. Careers that make good use of your integrity, such as the military and police force, are also good choices.

Leisure Time and Entertainment: You enjoy painting, gardening, fishing, reading the *New York Times*, and playing poker. (You could turn professional at the last.) Your tennis playing borders on the fanatical. You also enjoy just lying around in the hammock—it helps you think. You appreciate beauty very much, and you might consider starting a basket collection, if you haven't already. You know more about sports, music, and politics than do most of your acquaintances.

For vacation, try an excursion to Finland—the clean, simple living and breathtaking landscapes appeal to everything that is best in you.

Fashion Musts: Jewelry is one of your passions, and you like collecting a variety of interesting pieces. You like to wear amber, marcasite, pearls, and diamonds, of course. It goes without saying that you can tell the real thing from the fake at a glance. You tend to wear lots of rings and carry just a small clutch bag, perhaps a Kate Spade—your favorite. When it comes to clothing, you like to wear simple solids, for the most part—what better way to show off your fabulous jewelry collection?

Food Faves: Stir-fries, minestrone soup, and really good bread are some favorites. For dessert, anything with chocolate will pass muster—for a truly decadent experience, try a dark chocolate cheesecake with a morello cherry demi glaze.

Significant Others: You value kindness and affection more than anything else, and those are the qualities you look for in your significant other. With your charisma, you can attract just about anyone, but you do best with compassionate people like yourself who are not afraid to show their emotional side. Stay away from people who keep too many secrets.

Other Compatible Breed Personalities: Besides the Bullmastiff, you are compatible with French Bulldogs and Rottweilers.

Pet Peeve: You hate snoops.

Lucky Number: Numerological calculations for your breed reveal your lucky number to be 4.

Notable Bullmastiff People: Gary Larson, Sylvester Stallone

Chow Chow People

Personality and Character: There is a straightforward, beautiful intensity about you, and you have almost limitless energy. You also love a challenge, although you like to have a clear understanding of the facts before you will take a risk. Politics and social issues are your passions, and you pride yourself on your involvement. Along the same lines, you are attentive to others' needs, perceiving them even before they do themselves. You are also extremely well organized in almost every aspect of your life. In fact, you dislike chaos and can become infuriated when presented with it. Hardworking and self-sufficient, you definitely like to be in charge—there's no doubt about it. You prefer to work alone, although you can work with others if you have to. You just don't want to. (In your worst moments, you can be a bit difficult to get along with.)

Best Trait: Your best trait is your intensity.

Your Space: You are fond of expensive homes, and your kitchen is your favorite room, where you can whip up culinary masterpieces with magical ease. Sometimes you have to watch out for Chow Chow hair getting into the chow, but you're pretty obsessive about cleanliness, too. You need a lot of light in your life, and your ideal home has more glass than wall. Modern Scandinavian furniture inspires you.

Career: You would do well in any political, social, or humanitarian field. You are also very good with words and might do well in journalism.

Leisure Time and Entertainment: You like art that depicts your favorite breed, such as the portrait of the red Chow Chow Wang Lung, by American painter Gustav Muss-Arnolt. When it comes to music, you love Bob Dylan and Mozart equally, both of whom display musical intensity in different ways. You also enjoy comedic films, Martha Stewart, baseball, yoga, compliments, and above all else perhaps, a good back rub.

When it comes to vacation, you like to go where you can really see what is happening in a place—not just the obvious tourist spots. You arrange your own vacations (no tours or cruises) and like to poke around small villages and out-of-the-way beaches. Consider planning a trip to Mongolia!

Fashion Musts: Your trademark wardrobe item is your collection of fitted oxford shirts—just like Martha Stewart's. You're also a master of dressing to show your figure to its best advantage—complete with the perfect pair of strappy heels. For an elegant and sophisticated work look, try some pieces by label Ellen Tracy—they transition well to evening, so you'll save yourself some time and effort!

Food Faves: You love any kind of Chinese food, especially chow mein. For you, food is a window to the soul. You enjoy making your own noodles and gathering fresh vegetables and organic beef, chicken, or pork—and then putting them together in surprising but simple ways. You are creative at making interesting sandwiches as well. You are a marvelous cook—if you can imagine it, you can cook it.

Significant Others: Although you have no problems meeting people, it is hard for you to find the right one to settle down with permanently. Maybe this is because it's difficult for you to trust people at times. Look for someone who can appreciate your many good points.

Other Compatible Breed Personalities: Besides the Chow Chow, you are compatible with Boston Terriers and Miniature Pinschers.

Pet Peeve: You don't like it when people let things slide.

Lucky Number: Numerological calculations for your breed reveal your lucky number to be 8.

Notable Chow Chow People: Calvin Coolidge, Sigmund Freud, Martha Stewart

Valiant and Vivacious

Doberman Pinscher People

Personality and Character: Solid is the word for you—and so is energetic, creative, determined, conscientious, and loyal. You can also be extremely funny. Your intuition is always right on target, especially where your family is concerned, so pay heed to it. Generally, you are very content with your life and the choices you have made. You love hard work and are good with words—in fact, you have wonderful communication skills. You are an optimistic visionary and have very strong opinions about the way things ought to be done. You are high-minded, with the unique gift of being able to live in the world without getting caught up in it. You are also willing to make your dreams come true, and that's what separates you from a crowd of idealists. It's relatively easy for you to get close to others and depend on them—and you like having them depend on you.

Best Trait: Your conscientiousness is your best trait.

Your Space: You love the sights and sounds of the city. As to your home, you have done well with redecorating and making it a place of warmth and comfort. If you have a yard, plant a willow tree—its graceful beauty reflects your own. Or consider planting a moon garden for those lovely summer nights. But the winter is truly your time, even if the dog needs a jacket. In some mysterious way, you claim the darkest, coldest nights of the year as your own.

Career: You would do well in journalism, sales, or politics (perhaps not in elected office but definitely behind the scenes). You need a job where you can actually make things happen—preferably on your own terms.

Leisure Time and Entertainment: You're a fan of Beat Generation writers, Jack Kerouac in particular—his groundbreaking novel *On the Road* is one of your favorites. When it comes to favorite movie stars, you like Rudolf Valentino, James Cagney, and Jimmy Stewart; they appeal to your sweet, tough, and funny sides. You are also fond of competitive sports, especially individual sports like track, swimming, and kayaking. You love to take walks, especially at night—with your Doberman at your side, you're not afraid of anything.

For vacation, head for Kailua Beach, Hawaii, for its excellent windsurfing, kayaking, and water boarding. Don't look back—you need the break. If you want to go abroad, try something different and head to Morocco, where you can explore the casbah.

Fashion Musts: Accessories are your biggest fashion must, whether it be layers of fun necklaces or rows of bangles adorning each wrist. And besides jewelry, you know that nothing complements an outfit more than a great purse or the perfect pair of shoes. For a big splurge, try a pair of Manolo Blahnik heels—the higher the better!

Food Faves: Many Dobie owners like to eat on the run, so they prefer quick things—hot dogs, hamburgers, instant mashed potatoes—that can be hustled up in a matter of minutes. You like fast food, too, even though you know it isn't good for your figure. Luckily, your exercise drive takes care of most of that.

Significant Others: Headstrong, intense people often find you quite attractive and have a tendency to fall in love with you at first sight—your beautiful intensity draws them in. Your intimate relationships are a profound source of comfort to you, and you never hide your feelings or secrets from those you love. If you have children, you are an available, warm, and affectionate parent.

Other Compatible Breed Personalities: Besides the Doberman Pinscher, you are compatible with Flat-Coated Retrievers and German Shepherd Dogs.

Pet Peeve: You hate paying taxes.

Lucky Number: Numerological calculations for your breed reveal your lucky number to be 2.

Notable Dobie People: Sandra Bullock, Mariah Carey, Rudolf Valentino

Valiant and Vivacious

Fox Terrier People

Personality and Character: You love your life, and you have a very distinctive viewpoint on it. You are a happy, multitalented individual who can handle a lot of tasks at once. You are also witty and fun loving. You handle responsibility well, but if things go wrong, you can have a bit of a hot temper. With your irreverent sense of humor, you are a lot of fun to be around. You can be somewhat shy—you are certainly never one to show off—but only your nearest and dearest friends know this. Rather than talk about yourself all the time, you would rather let others talk about themselves. You are also a completely honest person—you would never read someone's diary or mail, for instance. You also wouldn't lie even to get yourself out of trouble. When things seem to be going wrong in your life, your optimism helps put you in a better frame of mind.

Best Trait: Your immense love of life—it shows through in everything you do.

Your Space: Your favorite rooms are the bedroom and bathroom, as these are your "private" spaces were you can express your own taste in a way that you can't in more public rooms. Your home is quite charming, filled with cool-toned decorating colors (blue is a favorite), windows, and lots of books. You prefer inexpensive replaceable furniture to classics because this allows you to change things around—which you love. Your garden is also a favorite place for you—you enjoy digging as much as your dog does. Plant foxglove in his honor.

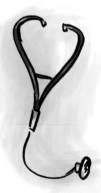

Career: You do best in careers that require fast action or multitasking. A job as a stockbroker, health-care professional, or in the publicity/marketing fields is a good possibility for you.

Leisure Time and Entertainment: You are an active person who doesn't like to sit around the house. Always on the go, you like nothing more than a night out at the movies, dancing, or barhopping. You like art that depicts your favorite breed, such as *The Totteridge XI*, by British classicist painter Arthur Wardle. You like Georgia O'Keefe, too. (You know she wasn't just painting flowers.) You're a fan of southern rock, especially Lynyrd Skynyrd.

You enjoy vacationing in places where you can do lots of things at the same time—and you wouldn't consider going anywhere without Internet access. You prefer to take your vacations in the United States—both coasts are especially exciting. The seashore is a perennial favorite, but you like going off-season best.

Fashion Musts: You tend to wear clothing that doesn't make you stand out too much, especially when it comes to colors: Neutrals and an overall monochromatic palette are your staples. For something a little different, express yourself with a beautiful fabric, like sateen, or an oversized bag. Try some separates by designer Alice Roi—her monochromatic pieces have a vintage feel to them and always manage to look interesting!

Food Faves: You like classic, all-American foods like pizza, hamburgers, and ribs—and there's nothing better than a pint of beer to top it all off.

Significant Others: You are totally idealistic when it comes to love. You and your mate become so truly one person that you feel like only half a person when you are apart. But watch your temper, or you could potentially lose someone who's very important to you.

Other Compatible Breed Personalities: Besides the Fox Terrier, you are compatible with Cairn Terriers and Pomeranians.

Pet Peeve: You can't stand it when people dwell on the negative.

Lucky Number: Numerological calculations for your breed reveal your lucky number to be 3.

Notable Fox Terrier People: Lucille Ball, Agatha Christie, Thomas Hardy, Herbert Hoover

Valiant and Vivacious

German Shepherd Dog People

Personality and Character: You are outgoing, direct, practical, and fearless, with a superior sense of right and wrong. In fact, there are no "exceptions to the rule" or gray areas with you, which sometimes puts you at risk of losing the good opinion of your friends. Extremely self-confident, you can be somewhat aloof to people you don't know. You choose your friendships very carefully, but those who earn your trust have it for life. You also have an authoritarian streak, which is something that can scare people away. Normally, you are a model of cool self-control. However, if someone angers you, they will seriously regret it. At the same time, you are tremendously intuitive and able to see goodness where others do not. Organized and efficient, you enjoy putting things in order; for example, you are very conscientious about sorting your laundry (a lost art, if truth be told).

Best Traits: Many people admire your directness and self-confidence.

Your Space: You want your home to be clean and functional, with lots of natural light. A great deal of glass and no window treatments is perfect for you. If possible, consider putting in a solarium. You even like outdoor restaurants! In your garden, try out some light-loving cactuses. Your ideal home is in the mountains, with a gorgeous view.

Career: German Shepherd Dog people excel in law enforcement—after all, German Shepherds were the first police dogs. Business is also a good choice because your strong ethical sense and self-confidence will help you succeed. Technology is a field where you excel as well, particularly because of your coolheadedness—when something goes wrong with the software, you are quietly setting about fixing it while everyone else is running around screaming.

Leisure Time and Entertainment: In the summer, an afternoon stroll along the boardwalk suits you wonderfully. In fact, you love to walk anywhere and are one of the few people who really enjoy sauntering about in the rain, no matter what others claim. You enjoy photography and sunrises, and there's nothing better, in your opinion, than spending as much time as possible outdoors. You are musical, too, and have a special talent for the piano and guitar. This musical talent helps you appreciate such legends as Led Zeppelin and the Doors. One of your favorite television series is *Rin Tin Tin*—a much better show than *Lassie*, you think.

You are rather a homebody when it comes to vacation, but you enjoy traveling in out-of-the-way places where you can be close to nature. A good backpacking trip in the mountains is perfect.

Fashion Musts: You tend to get bored with fashion rather quickly. In fact, the way something feels (comfortable!) is more important to you than how it looks or who made it, although classic sportswear by Tommy Hilfiger would suit your lifestyle perfectly. You have beautiful arms, so try to choose tops that show them off. You also consider makeup to be an annoyance, and you prefer a simple, no-nonsense hairstyle.

Food Faves: Outdoor, picnic-type foods are your favorites, especially German potato salad, almonds, cheese, and wine. One of your favorite snacks is beef jerky. (It's perfect for those backpacking trips.) You love a big breakfast to help get your day started—sausage, bacon, and scrambled eggs are favorites.

Significant Others: For you, love is an affair that lasts forever. You are totally loyal, even if the person ends up disappointing you. This is why it is critical for you to use both your intuition and your judgment in affairs of the heart. Your best mate is someone who is less opinionated than yourself.

Other Compatible Breed Personalities: Besides the German Shepherd Dog, you are compatible with Doberman Pinschers and Flat-Coated Retrievers.

Pet Peeve: You hate it when people don't say thank you.

Lucky Number: Numerological calculations for your breed reveal your lucky number to be 6.

Notable German Shepherd People: Bing Crosby, Billy Ray Cyrus, Steffi Graf, Jacqueline Kennedy, Franklin D. Roosevelt

Great Pyrenees People

Personality and Character: Reliable, decorous, confident, gentle, and affectionate are all adjectives that describe you. Learned and courteous, you give detailed, practical advice that others take (often without crediting you as the source, unfortunately). You are also helpful by nature and get along easily with other people. Indeed, your friends can always depend on you. Perseverance is your watchword—you never know when to give up, which is sometimes a good and sometimes a bad thing. Along the same lines, you set goals and do remarkably well at achieving them. You not only like to get things started, but you have the courage and integrity to see them through. One thing that most people don't realize about you is that you have an absolutely fantastic imagination and are wonderful with young children. (They are the first to sense your imaginative side.) You do have a tendency to lose things—or at least put them away and fail to remember where they are. (Remember the time you couldn't find the glasses that were right on your head?)

Best Trait: You are selfless, always wanting to help a friend in need.

Your Space: You are a great lover of books and libraries, filled with memorabilia. You require at least an hour to yourself every day to put your feet up and relax without people asking you to do things for them. You like birch and oak furniture, nothing too fancy. Your home is a little messy, but that's the way you like it.

Your Inner Dog

Career: You would be perfect at a career that involves children, perhaps teaching or running a day care center.

Leisure Time and Entertainment: Your favorite activities involve a lot of spectator sports. In fact, you like to sit back and observe, which may explain why parades, movies, and theater are so appealing to you. To indulge your imagination, you like to participate in fantasy games—and that includes fantasy sports. You also like art that features your favorite breed, such as the Great Pyrenees portraits by Edwin Megargee, which now hang in the American Kennel Club's museum.

For vacation, head for the Pyrenees—or indeed any other snow-capped mountains. Your ideal trip doesn't mean a lot of white-water rafting—you're happier enjoying the views, taking photos, and checking out the wildflowers.

Fashion Musts: You are fond of shopping and know how to take advantage of bargains and sales. Traditional, well-tailored clothing styles suit you well. (You also take excellent care of your clothes, and it shows.) Earth tones and natural fabrics define your wardrobe. Classic cashmere sweaters are one of your weaknesses—Hermès makes some beautiful ones. To add a little sparkle to your outfit, try a gold accessory, like an oversized bangle.

Food Faves: Ah, you can't resist that classic Pyrenees food, especially cassoulet (a delicious meat and white bean stew). When you're in the mood for more American fare, chicken, potatoes, and gravy suit you just fine. You also can't resist a glass of Madeira once in a while. You enjoy a good meal, but you definitely prefer other people to do the actual cooking!

Significant Others: You are family oriented and tend to be very sensible, even about romance. You are an excellent caretaker of everyone in your life, and you can be sure that happiness is in the cards for you.

Other Compatible Breed Personalities: Besides the Great Pyrenees, you are compatible with English Springer Spaniels and Newfoundlands.

Pet Peeve: The thing that annoys you most is people who complain.

Lucky Number: Numerological calculations for your breed reveal your lucky number to be 5.

Notable Great Pyrenees People: Mary W. Crane

Mixed-Breed People

Personality and Character: Your character is compassionate, genuine, and pure. You have the great gift of knowing what is truly important—of looking beneath the surface to find true value. Making the most out of life is extremely important to you, and you certainly lead a colorful existence, filled with fascinating experiences. Many people count you as a friend, and even though you never set out to be a leader, somehow you always attract followers. You are also extremely broad-minded, and not only are you imaginative as well, but you also have a lot of common sense, which can be a rather rare combination. Most important is your humanity—more than any other dog owner, you are likely to have adopted your dog from a shelter.

Best Trait: Your genuine nature shines through in everything you do.

Your Space: One word: outdoors! You love the beach in the summer and skiing in the winter, as long as you don't have to travel too far. Because your home is your favorite place, it can be a little messy (never dirty). You usually have more important things to worry about, like socializing.

Career: Teaching, health, or humanitarian work—careers that appeal to your caring and humanitarian side, which is really what you are all about.

Leisure Time and Entertainment: You enjoy getting out in the world and mixing with people. Simple, impromptu get-togethers are your favorite form of entertainment, but the best thing about you is that you are so spontaneous that you are willing to go anywhere or do anything at a moment's notice. You are not drawn to any specific activity as much as you are to being with your friends and enjoying yourself. Picnics, barhopping, vacationing together, going to concerts—it's all good.

When on vacation, you enjoy going to places that let you mix things up and do lots of different activities. That's why you love the Mediterranean region—it has everything.

Fashion Musts: Your fashion taste is eclectic—you like to mix and match vintage and modern pieces for a look that's all your own. For a similar style, try something by Anna Sui—she's able to make clothes from any decade look very "now." You don't normally buy expensive jewelry, instead preferring to collect antique costume pieces.

Food Faves: You like comfort foods—fried chicken and mashed potatoes are one of your favorites. Of course, you never forget the mixed greens salad or the gooey chocolate cake—prepared from a mix. Overall, you much prefer having a big family dinner to going out. Unless someone else pays; that's quite different, of course.

Significant Others: You are passionate and emotional, much more so than most people realize. When it comes to relationships, you care very little for the other person's outward appearance—you know it's the heart that counts. You need a solid, down-to-earth relationship that is all about equality and sharing, not dominance. And of course, you want someone with whom you can have a good time! Take care not to get involved with someone who will take you for granted and try to push you around. Be patient—the right person will appear.

Other Compatible Breed Personalities: Besides the mixed breeds, you are compatible with Great Danes and Vizslas.

Pet Peeves: Purists and stuck-up people annoy you the most.

Lucky Number: Average the lucky numbers for the breeds in your mix, if you know them. Otherwise, all numbers are equally lucky.

Notable Mixed-Breed People: Bill Cosby, Bob Dole, Bruce Lee, Mary Tyler Moore

Valiant and Vivacious

Petit Basset Griffon Vendéen People

Personality and Character: You are confident, happy, free spirited, and extroverted. Although you can be slightly aloof with those you don't know well, you are kindhearted, flexible, and social with friends. In fact, your passion, warmth, and sense of humor win the hearts of everyone around you. You hate to sit still, and your fun-loving and creative nature makes sure that doesn't happen too often. For you, life is one wild ride—you constantly seek what is new and exciting. You have faith in a peaceable world (even though you yourself can be charmingly hotheaded at times). You enjoy a good argument, but you also make up very quickly. You are also in the habit of completing what others leave undone. You have a natural business head—financially, you are a great saver. Your greatest failing is the difficulty you have setting goals and attaining them.

Best Trait: Your passion for life is your greatest asset.

Your Space: You love your bedroom, which you keep beautiful and well ordered. It is a vivid room, full of all the color and drama you expect in your life.

Career: Careers that employ your creativity, such as art and design, inventing, or acting, are perfect for you. You need to find a job in which your inventiveness is appreciated and can help atone for the difficulty you sometimes have with sticking to goals. People in the arts are used to dealing with people like you—so bursting with energy that it's hard to settle down at first. But when your interest is truly engaged, you are in for the long haul.

Leisure Time and Entertainment: Sunset on the beach is your favorite time and place. And no, you're not just sitting, staring into the sunset—you're swimming and playing volleyball, and then it's time for that big beach party. In sports you play to win—and it's charming. Even the people you beat don't seem to mind! You are having such a good time that your high spirits extend to everyone around you.

For vacation, you want an energizing trip that keeps you moving. You're one of the people who actually enjoys a city day tour. Closer to home, you like amusement parks with lots of thrill rides.

Fashion Musts: You have a wonderful "body sense" that seems to go well with everything—you just exude style. You are also often told that you look younger than you really are, and your fashion choices reflect your youthful looks. Natural fabrics and bold prints are hallmarks of your style, and designs by label Marni suit you perfectly.

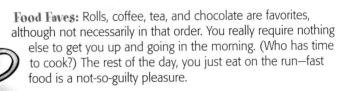

Food Faves: Rolls, coffee, tea, and chocolate are favorites, although not necessarily in that order. You really require nothing else to get you up and going in the morning. (Who has time to cook?) The rest of the day, you just eat on the run—fast food is a not-so-guilty pleasure.

Significant Others: You are devoted to your loved ones, especially your parents. For a significant other, you do best with someone who is sweet and gentle, to match your romantic side. If you get the wrong match, you could end up becoming too competitive and critical of your partner. Find someone who will give you the freedom you need to be truly happy.

Other Compatible Breed Personalities: Besides the Petit Basset Griffon Vendéen, you are compatible with Papillons and Skye Terriers.

Pet Peeve: Tailgaters are your biggest pet peeve.

Lucky Number: Numerological calculations for your breed reveal your lucky number to be 1.

Notable PBGV People: Mary Tyler Moore

Valiant and Vivacious

Rhodesian Ridgeback People

Personality and Character: You are emotional, imaginative, and adventurous, always ready to experience something new and exciting. You can speak intelligently on a wide variety of topics (especially social issues) and are in fact quite eloquent when the occasion calls for it. You also have the rare ability to accept authority without making too much of a fuss about it. However, you need intellectual freedom. You are quite fond of giving advice to others, which is usually appreciated—but not always. You never forget to return favors and are just as quick to give away money as advice. In fact, money is not important to you, and you are usually quite satisfied with what you earn, even though (or perhaps because) you are quite good at handling it. You do not get angry quickly, but when you do, you don't forgive easily. You can also be secretive and jealous, and it's difficult for others to know how you feel at times.

Best Trait: Your sense of adventure is your best trait.

Your Space: You are deeply in touch with nature, so you garden, especially in the fall. Try planting some flame lilies, acacias, and other native African plants to remind you of your dog's native land. You are also a big fan of "green living," and it shows in your home—you carefully conserve energy and space.

Career: Finance, law, or business is perfect for you,

especially when some speculation is called for—you like to take some risks. You can combine your financial acuity and imagination to make you a success at anything that requires both insight and good sense. And you have plenty of both.

Leisure Time and Entertainment: You are an expert at martial arts (and most other sports, in fact) and chess. You enjoy reading Doris Lessing's social works—she is from Zimbabwe (formerly known as Rhodesia). Indeed, you love reading books about Africa. In your low moments, nothing beats a good song by Elvis or Donny and Marie to cheer you up.

When it comes to vacation, there's always Zimbabwe. Indeed, an outdoor adventure anywhere on the African continent would be exciting. You often combine vacation with business and somehow always end up making money, even if that wasn't your original intent.

Fashion Musts: Show off your beautiful physique with simple, well-fitted clothing. Although you're not a fan of high fashion, you still enjoy looking good—casual wear just suits your lifestyle better. L.L. Bean makes hardy but modern clothing to add some style to even the roughest outdoor adventures. Purples and browns are great colors for you.

Food Faves: Food is usually the last thing on your mind, and you'd just as soon have takeout as anything else. Your idea of fine dining is pizza and red wine.

Significant Others: You hate conflict and seek an easygoing partner. Try to find someone who will take care of you without making too much of a fuss. In fact, you need someone who will really listen to you and give you strong emotional support.

Other Compatible Breed Personalities: Besides the Rhodesian Ridgeback, you are compatible with Neapolitan Mastiffs and Pembroke Welsh Corgis.

Pet Peeve: You hate waiting in line.

Lucky Number: Numerological calculations for your breed reveal your lucky number to be 9.

Notable Rhodesian Ridgeback People: Grace Kelly, Anthony Kiedis, Carl Lewis, Gabrielle Reece

Rottweiler People

Personality and Character: You have a strong sense of right and wrong, and you are invariably calm and courageous, with a great spirit of fair play. Sometimes you assume that the path ahead is going to be easier than it turns out to be. Consequently, you need to learn to relax and take a few moments to learn from the past. It is actually rather difficult to get you excited. You put the needs of others above yourself. You are a deep thinker and a freethinker, yet you are a great romantic as well. You have a strong need to control your life and your career—you hate fuss and chaos, and you dislike change. You are a hard worker (always have been) and started making money from an early age. On the negative side, some say that you have a short temper and are a little into one-upsmanship. Also, whenever things don't go your way, you tend to be moody and sulk. It's sometimes hard to tell because you are generally pretty quiet and reflective anyway. You love peace and harmony, but you have a temper that will flare up if you are attacked or criticized too sharply. Some Rottweiler people find it difficult to trust their own feelings—or to trust others.

Best Traits: You are hardworking and organized and can handle almost any situation.

Your Space: You're a fantastic cook, so the kitchen is your favorite room. (You have a fondness for granite countertops and gleaming stainless-steel appliances.) Your love of cooking includes barbecuing as well, especially in the summer. Your built-in outdoor grill is one of your prized possessions.

Career: You're versatile and can handle any career: social work (which appeals to your humanitarian side), engineering, law, architecture, sales, military, writing—really, you can succeed at anything you do. But you need to be in charge of your area—you have a hard time when you feel that your job is being unnecessarily interfered with.

Leisure Time and Entertainment: Outdoors, you love to cycle, often without a fixed destination. A solitary ramble along winding roads allows you to reflect on things. Indoors, you're a reader of the great classics. You love Cervantes—sometimes you feel like Don Quixote and sometimes not. You are quite fond of the opera because it appeals to your intellectual side. In lighter moments, you love a good game of Yahtzee or Monopoly. (After all, one cannot listen to arias 24 hours a day.)

For vacation, there is nothing like a trip to Germany, where you can not only visit the ancestral home of your favorite breed but also take in some Wagnerian opera.

Fashion Musts: You look great in timeless, tailored clothing in darker colors like black, dark brown, deep purple, and navy blue. Of course, you do brighten things up with hints of color, but it's always very subtle. To complement your wardrobe, try a piece by Helmut Lang—the epitome of minimalist chic, his well-fitted, sophisticated collection will flatter you well. If you decide to accessorize with jewelry, try an amber bracelet or ring—the color complements your dog.

Food Faves: You need plenty of food to fuel your thoughts. Although you have a preference for junk food, you try to avoid it for the sake of your health. You love beef and barbecue, but you are judicious about your portions.

Significant Others: You are uncomfortable in romantic situations unless you feel that you are in control. When you do fall in love, you are completely loyal, although you have a tendency to want to boss your partner around. Try not to choose someone who is too unpredictable—sudden changes make you nervous.

Other Compatible Breed Personalities: Besides the Rottweiler, you are compatible with Bullmastiffs and French Bulldogs.

Pet Peeve: You hate bad jokes.

Lucky Number: Numerological calculations for your breed reveal your lucky number to be 1.

Notable Rottweiler People: Leonardo DiCaprio, Carrie Fisher, Ken Griffey, Jr., Elton John, Will Smith

Valiant and Vivacious

Shar-Pei People

Personality and Character: Proud, brave, and passionate, you live for the moment and often get into trouble—but somehow you always manage to find a way out of it. You are action oriented, inventive, and hungry to experience everything in life, but somehow you manage to attempt it in a laid-back way. You don't like to commit yourself irrevocably to a decision because you feel that it ties you down. You have a good bit of artistic talent and are so good with body language that your slightest look or gesture can make your intentions known. You are also good at keeping a secret. You can be somewhat impatient at times—your fast-paced lifestyle can make it difficult for you to stay focused.

Best Trait: You are extremely spontaneous.

Your Space: You are inspired by the great outdoors, and your favorite "room" is really the patio, where you can be inside and outside at the same time, so to speak, and where you can relax. You use your artistic abilities to the utmost in creating a real outdoor "living room" where you can coexist with lots of potted plants and vines.

Career: A career in graphic design is just perfect for you. You can use your artistic ability but also connect with the exciting commercial world. You'd also be great in any business venture that combines art with the outdoors, such as wildlife photography.

Leisure Time and Entertainment: You don't confine yourself just to outdoor activities, although any kind of noncompetitive sport (hiking, jogging, kayaking) appeals to you. You're a person who enjoys creating music as well as listening to it—and there's nothing more fun than an impromptu jam session. Jazz is great, but it really doesn't matter as long as you're in the midst of it. It's the same with the other arts—you want to create as well as enjoy. You love writing off-the-cuff haiku and creating found art. You also enjoy dashing off to the movies at a moment's notice. Who cares what's playing? It's time to seize the moment!

When it comes to vacation, you love to travel to foreign lands and aren't happy unless every moment of the day is filled with excitement. You don't need anything planned out for you in advance, however. You prefer just renting a car or getting a rail pass and seeing what's at the next stop. Consider visiting China, the land of your dog, and don't forget to see the Great Wall.

Fashion Musts: Sometimes it's more important to you to be gorgeous than comfortable, especially because you have such a flair for fashion—and excellent taste, to boot. For a special night out, try a Nicole Miller party dress—in particular, try a print to liven things up. When it comes to colors that suit you, green is extremely flattering, especially when paired with copper bangles or dramatic drop earrings.

Food Faves: You enjoy Chinese food, but you like it takeout style, where you can select a vast number of things at a moment's notice. You know you are so impulsive that by the time you get home, you may not hanker for what you ordered—so just in case, you get a little bit of everything.

Significant Others: You love to flirt, and you hold the key to all hearts. A big danger when it comes to relationships is letting outside interests distract you from your main commitment. You're not faithless, but you *are* easily beguiled. Your love life thrives when you take risks—nothing really dangerous, of course, but perhaps a little harmless flirting to spice things up. You are a very good kisser.

Other Compatible Breed Personalities: Besides the Shar-Pei, you are compatible with Cocker Spaniels and Poodles.

Pet Peeve: You can't stand it when a roadmap isn't folded correctly.

Lucky Number: Numerological calculations for your breed reveal your lucky number to be 4.

Notable Shar-Pei People: Yul Brynner, Wayne Newton, Burt Reynolds, William Shatner, Steve Wozniak

Saint Bernard People

Personality and Character: You have a large and colorful personality and know how to put every second of your day to good purpose. Kind and selfless, you tend to put the needs of others before yourself; in fact, you are willing to help people and expect nothing in return. You are extremely loyal and proud of those you love—and protective of them, too. You come from a background of hard work and self-reliance, although you may have a tendency to bite off more than you can chew. You are extremely good at understanding concepts and employing them, although sometimes you take too long to make a decision. Living in the present moment, you are enthusiastic and full of zest, and you are always ready for unexpected events. In fact, you are fascinated by what goes on around you and are highly observant. Your biggest fault is blaming others, and you need to more clearly define your long-term goals.

Best Trait: Your best trait is your ability to live in the present moment.

Your Space: You like a casual living space, with comfortable, plushy furniture that gives everyone a feeling of home. You enjoy a free-flowing interior with high ceilings (you do have a big dog, after all). Although you don't mind being thrifty at times, life's comforts are also very important to you—and you don't skimp on them. A good view is essential to your happiness.

Career: Running a bed-and-breakfast in the Alps would be a dream job for you. You might also consider writing (for the fun of it) or being a drug safety specialist (for the money). Or stick to inn-keeping and have both. Some Saint Bernard people also go in for border patrol or customs jobs.

Leisure Time and Entertainment: In the summertime, you're a tennis aficionado, and in the winter, you like to ski—preferably in Switzerland, near the St. Bernard Pass. (The views are wonderful.) You are artistic and love art that features your favorite breed, especially Maud Earl's *I Hear a Voice*, featuring a Saint Bernard. (You'd like to hang it in your home but would have to cover it with glass to protect it from drool.) Of course, one of your favorite television shows is *Topper*, which featured Neil, the Saint Bernard.

Besides Switzerland, you might also enjoy visiting less-traveled parts of the world—perhaps tramping about the wilder parts of Scandinavia or trekking through the Baltic countries. You like to be self-reliant, and you regard the best vacations as places to test your ability to meet a challenge.

Fashion Musts: Fashion is not a top priority for you—you just want to be comfortable! You want informal clothes that you can actually walk in, even in deep snow. The L.L. Bean catalog is where you can find the most utilitarian clothing for your lifestyle. When it comes to the most flattering colors for you, bright is best, especially yellow.

Food Faves: Brandy is a favorite, with or without a keg around your neck. For more solid fare, nothing beats breakfast—muffins, buttermilk pancakes, cinnamon rolls, maple syrup, strawberry preserves, raspberry kringles . . . yummy. When you're finished, you can start on lunch.

Significant Others: Without a stable, steady relationship, Saint Bernard people often feel emotionally insecure. When it comes to romance, you are the idealistic type, and you are most romantic when you are at home. Remember not to get so busy at work that you ignore your family!

Other Compatible Breed Personalities: Besides the Saint Bernard, you are compatible with Beagles and Irish Setters.

Pet Peeve: You hate when people read to you.

Lucky Number: Numerological calculations for your breed reveal your lucky number to be 8.

Notable Saint Bernard People: Betty White

Chapter 4

Smart and Sassy

Airedale Terrier People • Australian Shepherd People • Beagle People • Border Collie People • Borzoi People • Collie People • Designer Dog People • English Springer Spaniel People • Finnish Spitz People • Jack Russell Terrier People • Lhasa Apso People • Poodle People • Shetland Sheepdog People • Siberian Husky People • Whippet People

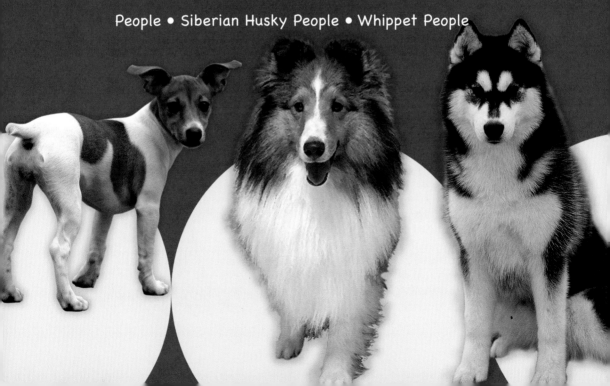

Personality and Character: You have a magical mind. You are intelligent, extremely organized, and feel most comfortable in theoretical conversations, especially those with a mystical twist. (You know very well that there's an alien at Roswell, and you aren't going to let anyone talk you out of it.) You also like having your palm read. You never forget a favor—or an insult. You want to provide the best possible life for yourself and your loved ones, and you are very interested in their security. You have a great deal of optimism about the future, and that is one of your most appealing characteristics. You're also a bit of a free spirit. You don't get resentful easily, and your temper builds slowly—but when it does, others should watch out!

Best Trait: You are a wonderful storyteller.

Your Space: You love the ocean but are equally at home in inland valleys and the open, windswept moors—any place where you can enjoy the rugged comfort that is second nature to you. You are definitely a "cabin" sort of person. In the house, your favorite room is the kitchen, where you are fond of sorting out your spice rack. Some of those herbs are magical, after all, and you want them where you can find them. You also require space for meditation and relaxation, and your home has many comfortable places for people to sit.

Career: Because you're such a free and airy spirit, with a penchant for the magical, look for a career that pulses with the spirit of the New Age: A career in spiritual health, psychic readings, or New Age merchandising is perfect for you.

Leisure Time and Entertainment: It's no accident that you love the mysterious, darkly magical works of the Brontë sisters (who, incidentally, come from the Aire Valley). You enjoy New Age music but love classical composer and Aire Valley native Frederick Delius best of all—his sensuous, elusive music always touches your heart. You are also fond of Internet shopping and are known for lavishing your dog with gifts.

When it comes to vacation, you are happy lying around on a hammock or exploring scenic sites close to home, preferably by bike. You also like relaxing over a candlelit dinner—followed by sitting on the verandah. If you do venture abroad, say to South America or even the Aire Valley, you'd enjoy doing the same things—for you, vacation is all about relaxation!

Fashion Musts: You do best in lightweight cotton fabrics—nothing to weigh you down! Bright colors are especially flattering on you, perhaps because they reflect your optimistic spirit. For a night out or special date, wear something flirty and feminine, perhaps a dress by designer Tracy Reese. Otherwise, you're comfortable in jeans and a simple tee.

Food Faves: You are well aware of the electromagnetic energy within foods, and you like to power up with strong, energy-packed meats like roast beef, pork, and lamb. For dessert, nothing's better than a delicious slice of chocolate or pecan pie, which appeal to your sweet side.

Significant Others: You need to learn to balance your love of freedom with your desire for commitment. You love a relationship in which feelings are fully shared, and you crave the company of someone who is enchanted by magic and fantasy of all sorts, just as you are.

Other Compatible Breed Personalities: Besides the Airedale Terrier, you are compatible with Finnish Spitzes and Shetland Sheepdogs.

Pet Peeve: You hate receiving age-related birthday cards—you're ageless anyway.

Lucky Number: Numerological calculations for your breed reveal your lucky number to be 5.

Notable Airedale Terrier People: Ty Cobb, Bo Derek, Theodore Roosevelt, John Wayne, Woodrow Wilson

Personality and Character: You are charismatic and fun-loving, and you always live in the present. In fact, you have no trouble breaking with the past, and you never carry "baggage." Sometimes you become completely engaged in whatever you are doing, so much so that you can lose track of the time. Proud and self-confident, you like to keep your options (and mind) open—however, your ego can lead you to disaster if you are not careful. You are also cheerful, a great conversationalist (although your sense of humor can be somewhat dark), and dependable, earning the respect of friends and family. However, you can be more defensive than you need to be, especially when it comes to family affairs. Prevent conflict in these matters by being more upfront about your personal concerns.

Best Trait: You have the ability to compromise and remain independent at the same time.

Your Space: Actually, you like places away from home—you like to be on the move—and the beach is one of your favorite spots. At home, you have an eclectic decorating style, and your dwelling is decorated with objects from all your travels. You like "fun" design colors, like turquoise and fuchsia. Your house is usually spotless.

Career: Because you enjoy travel so much, you should think about a career with an international flavor—one that allows you to be on the move. A job with a

Your Inner Dog

multinational company might be just the ticket as you hop from one headquarters to another. You would be excellent at taking a down-on-its-luck segment of a corporation and giving it wings.

Leisure Time and Entertainment: You're a big reader, and you prefer short stories, thrillers, and action literature. (You were one of the few people in your high school class who actually liked *Moby Dick*.) When outdoors, you are a big fan of extreme sports, like rock climbing and snow boarding. You also dance a mean tango. (Nothing keeps you moving faster than that!) For vacation, a trip to Australia's outback has always appealed to you. And when you go, you won't stop until you get to Perth.

Fashion Musts: You know all the current fashion trends—right up to the minute, actually. You're never afraid to try the newest and most daring fashions, especially if it's something by an avant-garde designer, like Vivienne Westwood. In fact, you despise anything with a tailored, conservative look unless it is in fashion at the moment. You can also wear a hat perfectly, which is not as easy as it looks.

Food Faves: In honor of your Shepherd, you do have a fondness for shepherd's pie and biscuits—they fit well into a boxed lunch that you can take with you wherever you go. And since there's always something to celebrate, you love to have a good bottle of wine or champagne on hand.

Significant Others: You are a generous and loving mate, but sometimes it's difficult for you to trust another person in a relationship. You have a tendency to keep secrets from even those nearest and dearest to you. You are especially attracted to people who make good dance partners, and you want someone easygoing who can handle your freewheeling personality.

Other Compatible Breed Personalities: Besides the Australian Shepherd, you are compatible with Golden Retrievers and Miniature Schnauzers.

Pet Peeve: You hate it when people are sluggish.

Lucky Number: Numerological calculations for your breed reveal your lucky number to be 1.

Notable Australian Shepherd People:
Sally Field, Steve Jobs, Demi Moore, Tim Robbins, Susan Sarandon

Personality and Character: You are the epitome of congeniality, there's no doubt about it—you get along with just about everyone. Your nature is extremely peaceful, and you are interested in serving others. You are motivated by your dreams and ideals. Always poised, you are an independent and savvy individual who works hard to achieve your goals—and you bring a positive attitude to any situation. You are slow to make judgments about right and wrong, which is sometimes good—and sometimes not. You just find it difficult to make a decision at times for fear of being wrong. You've also been accused of talking a lot and not saying very much (which is not true—you have a lot to say!).

Best Trait: Your best trait is your utter, utter charm.

Your Space: You love open spaces, and your home is imaginative, even inspired. Your favorite colors are sea green, light blue, and yellow. You love to entertain, and your home is comfortable but not always company ready. You never hang around with snobs, though, so no one cares if the place isn't perfect. Besides, your warm nature is reflected in every piece of furniture. Your home is truly everyone's home.

Career: So what if you didn't make it into the top ten percent of your class? You've got what it takes to make it in the real world. Your ambition is to be a flying ace, journalist, or great novelist, and if you haven't managed to do it yet, you soon will.

Your Inner Dog

Leisure Time and Entertainment: You don't care what you do, as long as you have plenty of company and you can be outside. Team sports are favorites of yours, and you love things like bowling, where you can not only participate but gab and gossip with everyone. Beagle owners are also very likely to join a writers' group, where they can share their own work and talk about others' as well. You read everything but have a particular interest in graphic novels—and of course, your favorite reads include the *Peanuts* comics, featuring that famous Beagle, Snoopy.

When it comes to vacation, you should definitely consider a trip to the Galapagos Islands, the way Darwin did aboard the HMS *Beagle*. You also enjoy just being outside at night, looking up at the stars. This is yet another reason why an island vacation is so exciting—away from the city lights, you can actually see what's out there.

Fashion Musts: Beagle people tend to be fans of "natural" fashion. In fact, more than one of you is a nudist. (With your tough, trim little figure you can handle it!) For those Beagle people who prefer to wear clothes, perhaps donning more natural fabrics, like cotton, would appeal. Or try some animal-friendly clothing—Stella McCartney's line is completely animal-free.

Food Faves: In general, Beagle owners like everything, especially if they can carry it around in a large bowl and chomp on it outside while chatting to their many friends. You especially like all kinds of party food—peanuts (of course!), chips, pretzels, you name it—it's so great to share, and that's what you do best. Food is never the focus, though (the way it probably is for your dog)—it's the friends, the company, and the conversation.

Significant Others: You are a loving person but often need to "get away" for a few hours or even days. It's the wanderlust—you actually would be just as delighted if your significant other accompanied you (and that's the kind of person your prefer: a fellow wanderer). You don't really like bossy people, though; you're definitely attracted more to the Charlie Browns of this world than to the Lucys.

Other Compatible Breed Personalities: Besides the Beagle, you are compatible with Irish Setters and Saint Bernards.

Pet Peeve: You hate it when people call too late at night or too early in the morning.

Lucky Number: Numerological calculations for your breed reveal your lucky number to be 5.

Notable Beagle People: Charlie Brown, James Herriot, Lyndon B. Johnson, Barry Manilow, Charles M. Schulz

Personality and Character: You have a tremendous amount of energy and are an extremely intelligent and successful person. Strong willed, hyped up, and ambitious, you don't have time for small talk—it's full steam ahead all the way! You are a confident and dynamic individual, and subtlety is definitely not your strong suit. In fact, you have a strong belief that you are fated for success, and you are probably right—but you are also quite willing to help fate along. You like to think of new ways of doing things and are much more imaginative than most of your friends. It's important for you to find a healthy balance between work and play, which is not always easy for you. Also, although you have the best intentions, you have a tendency to make decisions for other people that are not yours to make.

Best Trait: You're able to bring others to action through your verve and enthusiasm.

Your Space: Your home design is simple and efficient, and you are so good at organizing closets that it's scary. Your favorite room is your living room—after all, living is what you do best! It is a serene sanctuary for your hectic life but practical, too. When decorating, you like to express yourself with different patterns, colors, and textures. Some people might find your taste a bit theatrical, but it is so you. Style, after all, is as important as function.

Career: A career in a high-powered, high-stress job, like in the stock market, is perfectly suited to your personality. But no matter what you choose to do, you won't stop until you're in the highest echelon. You were born to take a leadership role.

Leisure Time and Entertainment: Activities that take you out of the house and into the great outdoors are your favorites, especially biking, rollerblading, and golf. You can walk or even jog all day and never get tired. Cerebral games like golf and chess appeal to you, and you're quite good at solving a Rubik's cube. You also have a great deal of respect for Benjamin Franklin, a multitalented genius much like yourself. In addition, you like to discuss politics, especially when it comes to protecting our borders.

For vacation, try the borderlands between Scotland and England. For the most part, though, you actually don't care that much where you go as long as there is plenty to do. Without a thorough plan, you may find yourself creating your own activities, something that has gotten you into trouble more than once.

Fashion Musts: When it's cold out, it's no surprise that you like to keep warm with a nice fleece jacket. You are also wonderful in a plunging neckline, something to show off your svelte figure. And believe it or not, you're someone who can actually wear lace without looking ridiculous. Designer Pamella Roland makes some beautiful dresses that combine a plunging neckline with touches of lace—they'd be perfect for your figure.

Food Faves: Lamb is one of your favorite foods, naturally. For dessert, cherry and pumpkin pie (the latter with a ginger cookie crust) are near the top of your list. You are also known for making the best cocktails and party punches in town—and you never give away the recipe.

Significant Others: You can be a bit of a loner romantically, although you thrive in social situations. You need someone who will accept you unequivocally, who will stick by you no matter what, and who will also respect and admire you. You have a tremendous capacity to love and be loved, but that doesn't always translate into a stable partnership. Find someone with similar interests, and you'll do just fine.

Other Compatible Breed Personalities: Besides the Border Collie, you are compatible with Maltese and Whippets.

Pet Peeve: Being bored is your biggest pet peeve.

Lucky Number: Numerological calculations for your breed reveal your lucky number to be 1.

Notable Border Collie People: Courteney Cox, Ellen DeGeneres, Kiefer Sutherland

Personality and Character: Brilliant, original, and iconoclastic, you are still a modest, even humble person. In fact, you always seem to be the center of attention, although you are not flashy. Your strength of character (especially your honesty) and strong work ethic come through in all circumstances. Perhaps you are not as flexible as others, for you do insist upon your own point of view. You also have a true love of learning and are genuinely curious and interested in the world. Nothing makes you happier than learning something new—and you seem to know everything! You don't jump to conclusions and always require a solid foundation of fact upon which to base your decisions. People consider you a highly rational thinker (although you can be a tad bit sentimental). You are very loving, with powerful feelings, but sometimes give off a "chilly" air at first. You are a strong environmentalist.

Best Trait: Your best trait is your integrity.

Your Space: Your favorite room is your bathroom—after all, that's where you start and end the day. Your bath is a beautiful retreat and a delight to the senses, for you can evoke your unusual taste to create something really special. You are not afraid to try dramatic colors and glass mosaics. Use bronze and color accents to create a spectacular effect, creating a dramatic room that simply shimmers.

Career: Teaching would be a good career for you. You are able to find creative and unusual ways to approach your subjects, and you have the ability to inspire your students. Borzoi people also make pioneering and trendsetting artists.

Your Inner Dog

Leisure Time and Entertainment: Many Borzoi people are highly musical—many even have perfect pitch. You often prefer classical music, particularly passionate, iconoclastic composers such as Alexander Scriabin. You also enjoy reading, especially those great (but long) Russian novels, like Tolstoy's *War and Peace* and Dostoevsky's *Crime and Punishment*. Borzoi people make fine bicyclists and good runners, especially at sprint distances—the 100-meter is your favorite.

For vacation, consider visiting Russia, the homeland of the Borzoi—especially the countryside. You also love ecotours of all kinds and not simply to the packaged, well-traveled spots. You enjoy simply hiking out on your own, accompanied by your quiet, well-behaved dog whenever possible.

Fashion Musts: You are stylish and sophisticated. Subtly glamorous clothing with clean, flowing lines that fit well to the body suits you best. If you're looking for a designer piece (and most fashion-minded Borzoi people are), try something by Chanel, which embodies traditional elegance at its best. You are also exceptionally talented with makeup, although most Borzoi people don't really need it.

Food Faves: It's no surprise that you enjoy Russian favorites like borscht and vodka. But you have that sweet side of you to indulge as well. Caviar is for parties, of course, but when spending a quiet evening at home, you like to make little Russian pastries crammed with potatoes, meat, cabbage, or cheese. Candy is a favorite—you love that sugar rush!

Significant Others: You tend to be drawn to quiet, rather reserved people—flashy extroverts are a definite turnoff. You don't need anyone too complicated, but prefer someone with interests similar to your own who can be a true partner. With the right partner, you'll simply soar. Alas, a few Borzoi people tend to work too hard and so may neglect their mates somewhat.

Other Compatible Breed Personalities: Besides the Borzoi, you are compatible with Brussels Griffons and Jack Russell Terriers.

Pet Peeve: Badly behaved children are a huge pet peeve.

Lucky Number: Numerological calculations for your breed reveal your lucky number to be 4.

Notable Borzoi People: Captain E.J. Smith of the *Titanic*, Grand Duke Nicholas Nicolaievich of Russia

Personality and Character: You are poised, dignified, and ambitious, with strongly realized goals—and you do not like to be thwarted. As an intellectual, you can seem a little detached; perhaps your thinking is a bit too abstract. However, you do have a wonderful intuitive sense—no one can deny that. You are superior at analyzing any situation (or person) and can communicate extremely well in nonverbal as well as verbal ways. You are both charming and witty. You are also a good citizen and can somehow always attract the right people to get things done. In fact, you're always the first person to help people out when they are short of funds. You are a rock upon which others lean, but you are not particularly interested in controlling others. (Leave that to your dog.) At times, you have been known to have a rather sharp temper, but it is to your credit that it is never over anything trivial.

Best Trait: Not only can you visualize your goals well, but you usually achieve them, too.

Your Space: Your home is your castle, and you just love to be there. It's designed along classic, traditional lines and so has a lot of granite and Victorian touches. You really admire Scotland's famous Hill House, designed by architect Charles Rennie Mackintosh (which is as close to a real castle as a home can be), with its heavy walls, minimal outside ornamentation, and sturdy, sober construction. Inside it's warm, carefully decorated, and almost exotic—just like you.

Career: Look for a career in law, civil service, or the mechanical fields. In other words, your career choices are pretty much unbounded, for you bring dedication and ability to any profession. In all these jobs, you have an opportunity to make a real difference in people's lives. You are also very good at dealing with the public and would even make a good ambassador.

Leisure Time and Entertainment: You are interested in learning about Scottish sports and activities, like ax throwing and falconry. Scotland is, after all, the home of your favorite breed. You can even play the harp, but you won't go as far as the bagpipes. You like books and movies that feature your favorite breed, especially the book *Lassie* and the movie *Lassie Come Home.* (You always cry.) With your keen sense of detail and ability to see the whole picture, you also make a terrific pool player. For a more active adventure, you enjoy cycling, hiking, and running. All these things give you a chance to think.

   When it comes to vacation, Scotland is an ideal spot; its stark beauty gives you a chance to meditate and be creative. However, you have so much strength within yourself that you don't really need to go anywhere to do those things.

Fashion Musts: You are always impeccably dressed, especially for work. Jil Sander suits, with their modern, minimalist tailoring, are perfect for the office and flatter your figure. When it comes to jewelry, you'd rather save your money and buy the real thing—no costume pieces for you! Precious stones in understated settings, like a smaller ring or tasteful earrings, work with your elegant sense of style.

Food Faves: You enjoy delicious but fuss-free foods. Crock-Pot dinners, hearty casseroles, and wonderful soups suit you to a tee. Fruits, especially cantaloupe, are also favorites. You love M&M's; just sorting them out by color is kind of like herding sheep.

Significant Others: Your love is enduring, and you are totally devoted to your family. Your ideal mate has the common sense, pragmatic outlook, and deep feelings that you have yourself. Sometimes you can become irrationally attracted to someone who is your complete opposite, but be careful—while these types of relationships often have happy endings, they don't always.

Other Compatible Breed Personalities: Besides the Collie, you are compatible with American Staffordshire Terriers and Bichons Frises.

Pet Peeve: You hate dirty bathrooms in public places.

Lucky Number: Numerological calculations for your breed reveal your lucky number to be 2.

Notable Collie People: Calvin Coolidge, Lyndon B. Johnson, Marilyn Monroe

Personality and Character: You just are different from the average Joe, and you know it. Life is a gamble, and you fear nothing. You love the world and enjoy a good time as much as you love work, and in many ways you stay a child at heart. You are original as well and enjoy coming up with new theories. You are also kindhearted and generous but sometimes fail to take the initiative, even when you should. At the same time, though, you have an able intellect and tremendous creative potential—and you love nothing more than an exciting challenge to test your mind. You do have a little difficulty reading people and are so trusting that you can be taken in by frauds and fakes. One of your main flaws is that you try too hard to keep up with the Joneses, sometimes not realizing how much you already have.

Best Trait: Your passionate spirit is your best trait.

Your Space: Your favorite room is the kitchen, where you can indulge your taste for unusual combinations, both food-wise and in terms of your decor. It is truly the place to experiment to reveal the real (and very unusual) you. You like to decorate with flowers, especially unusual, oversized, flowering plants. You are especially fond of using handcrafted mosaic medallions in both the flooring and countertops for a unique touch. You do not attempt to impress people with your great taste, even though you invariably do just that.

Career: You excel in professions that make use of your drive and intelligence. Something in biotechnology, the life sciences, or any other field that combines science and creativity is just up your alley.

Leisure Time and Entertainment: You enjoy combining work and pleasure—for instance, you like golfing enough to combine it with making a business deal. You also enjoy musical comedy, especially Broadway shows, and other forms of entertainment that combine several art forms. Your reading tastes bend toward the practical—you enjoy how-to books that teach you skills you can incorporate into your own life. In music, you enjoy creative groups that can combine several different genres and yet somehow manage to create their own sound.

When it comes to vacation, you like carefully crafted trips that combine unusual features, like perhaps camping during the day and clubbing at night. Whatever you do, you always look for that "best of both worlds" idea. Try South America or Australia, both of which offer a lot of variety.

Fashion Musts: You like interesting style combinations that most people find unusual—but you manage to pull it off. Nicolas Ghesquiere's avant-garde designs for Balenciaga perfectly match your fashion-forward sense of style. Large flowered prints, futuristic silhouettes, and a great shoe get you noticed!

Food Faves: You enjoy carefully crafted meals comprising unusual combinations of ingredients: carrots and sugar, coffee and chocolate, tomatoes and sugar, apples and vanilla—you name it, you've tried it! (At least you don't have to worry about anyone else eating your food.) You also like a simple chocolate chip cookie now and then. You love to cook and know how to set a beautiful holiday table. You also really know how to clean silver.

Significant Others: It seems that several people are always interested in you at once—but we each must bear our burdens. You're capable of any effort, any sacrifice on behalf of your loved ones—as long as it does not violate your ethics. If your relationship with a significant other goes sour, it can send you into a serious depression.

Other Compatible Breed Personalities: Besides the designer dog, you are compatible with Chinese Cresteds and Lhasa Apsos.

Pet Peeve: Unemotional people drive you crazy.

Lucky Number: Your lucky number depends on what kind of designer dog you have. Average the lucky numbers for the breeds from which your dog is derived.

Notable Designer Dog People: Jennifer Aniston, James Gandolfini, Jake Gyllenhaal, Jessica Simpson, Tiger Woods

Personality and Character: You are more interested in generalities than in details and enjoy looking for theories to back up your observations. In fact, theory in general fascinates you, especially when it comes to the sciences. Your personality is often described as "larger than life," and you like to be the center of attention. At the same time, you are stable, kind, and affectionate and are actually rather easygoing in social relationships. Diplomacy is the key to your working style. You have high self-esteem and very few self-doubts; you are definitely your own person. You have a great understanding of humanity, but you insist on high standards for yourself and others. Despite this admirable trait, you've been known to obscure the facts a time or two.

Best Trait: Your best trait is your stable, affectionate personality.

Your Space: In your home, you like hardwood floors and bright area rugs, and your decor also features a lot of glass, metals, and pottery. The bathroom is your favorite room—it's not a utilitarian necessity but a center for self-renewal and pampering. Granite countertops, which are not only handsome but easy to clean, are a must, as are bowl-shaped sinks and real furniture. (No metal-rimmed medicine cabinets for you.) You also take care to make the entryway of your home stunning—you need to because you spend so much time going in and out.

Career: You work best in a job where you have lots of contact with the public. You'd be great in sales or customer service—especially dealing with luxury merchandise. A career in the sciences would also suit you well because of your love of theory and observation.

Your Inner Dog

Leisure Time and Entertainment: In your leisure time, you rather enjoy a little competition and challenge. However, you mostly prefer to challenge yourself—you may take up bungee jumping or skydiving. Because you tend to be lucky, you also indulge in a little gambling now and again. You can become very sentimental about sports and get emotional after a big win or loss by your favorite team. Your musical tastes run to whoever is the reigning diva of the moment—you love Mariah Carey, especially.

For vacation, you don't want to lie around on the beach or stay in some crumbling villa. Look for a sociable, sophisticated, and stimulating atmosphere, like Rio, London, or Paris. You want the museums, but you like to shop, too. At the end of the day, you want to kick back in your very old-world, one-of-a kind, sophisticated boutique hotel.

Fashion Musts: When it comes to fashion, solid colors and a tailored, modern look are your trademark. Designers like Richard Tyler, with his emphasis on well-fitted, elegant pieces, appeal to your style sensibilities. Cool colors, especially blues and purples, look great on you. Diamonds are the perfect accessory.

Food Faves: You are among the few dog owners who can actually stand liver, although you prefer a simple all-American burger (on a whole-grain bun, of course). You like anything salty as a snack, especially olives and pickles—they seem to wake up your brain.

Significant Others: You wear your heart on your sleeve, but you are wise enough to choose a person with whom you are good friends first before beginning an intimate, romantic relationship. Choose someone who also gets along with your friends—and your dog, of course.

Other Compatible Breed Personalities: Besides the English Springer Spaniel, you are compatible with Great Pyrenees and Newfoundlands.

Pet Peeve: You hate annoying bumper stickers.

Lucky Number: Numerological calculations for your breed reveal your lucky number to be 5.

Notable English Springer People: Jimmy Buffet, George and Barbara Bush

Personality and Character: Some people call you a lone wolf, although in some ways you are more fox-like than wolfish. (Perhaps you take after your dog.) You can be reticent, even rather chilly. (You have rather a passion for silence.) Indeed, you may not be in tune with the feelings of others, and you don't always interact with them as well as you could. However, deep down you are kind, funny, and humble. You are a brilliant thinker and a seeker of truth. You are not one to dally over unimportant things. You thrive on beauty, and creativity is the key to your working style. You keep your ear to the ground and know what is happening, and it is very important for you to be in touch with nature. You are also rather materialistic—not in a bad sense but in the sense that you want to enjoy beautiful things (like your beautiful dog).

Best Trait: Your quiet confidence is your best trait.

Your Space: You are definitely into Nordic chic, with lots of Norse and Celtic elements woven into your design choices, and your home is your canvas. Your home decor embodies this typically minimalist vision, but the few things you have are not only rare and expensive but well made and practical for everyday use. However, you are not wedded to traditional shades of off-white—you like to indulge your passion for color. A sauna is a must for you.

Career: You'd be great in the biology field or any other scientific endeavor. Your single-minded passion for truth and profound thinking skills make you a natural in this field.

Leisure Time and Entertainment: You are passionate about books, and *An Inconvenient Truth*, by Al Gore, is among your favorites. After all, Finland has been more affected than most places by global warming. As a child, you were quite a fan of the classics, including *The Secret Garden*. You also enjoy quiet, noncompetitive activities that you can indulge on your own, including sewing, fishing, and gardening. You're also pretty good at doing imitations of other people.

For vacation, visit Finland for the time of your life. Actually, any place that's cool, quiet, and above all, beautiful, would suit you just fine. Alaska, Maine, and Scotland offer similar frigid delights.

Fashion Musts: Dressing loudly is not your style—you like to wear simple, unfussy clothing that uses natural fabrics, especially pieces by Eileen Fisher. Comfort is key! Although you tend to wear more subdued colors on an everyday basis, try to change it up once in a while with a geometric design, stripes, or a bold hue. A comfortable ballet flat can also add a splash of color and style to an otherwise quiet ensemble.

Food Faves: Loyal to your dog's country of origin, you like to sample Finnish specialties like Karelian pasties (rye crust with a rice filling), *mämmi* (an Easter dessert with orange peel, molasses, and rye flour), *kalakukko* (fish inside a loaf of bread), cabbage rolls, pickled herring, and smoked fish. You also love mashed potatoes and sautéed reindeer . . . but then who doesn't?

Significant Others: Although you tend to spend quite a bit of time by yourself, you still value relationships and are able to deeply and emotionally commit to someone. When you enter into a serious relationship with another person, you want it to last forever. You see qualities in your partner that no one else sees, and you treasure them.

Other Compatible Breed Personalities: Besides the Finnish Spitz, you are compatible with Airedale Terriers and Shetland Sheepdogs.

Pet Peeve: People who feel sorry for themselves annoy you.

Lucky Number: Numerological calculations for your breed reveal your lucky number to be 7.

Notable Finnish Spitz People: Lady Kitty Ritson

Personality and Character: You are strongly imaginative, clever, intense, and loyal. You are interested in serving others, but in this regard it is easy for others to take advantage of you. In fact, you may be tempted to give loyalty to those who do not deserve it, and you always seem to be pursuing some lost cause. Stories of other people's problems always manage to touch your heart. You hate theory and analysis, although you are inquisitive and enjoy learning. In fact, your curiosity can lead to recklessness and get you into a dangerous situation. You are a hard worker and don't tolerate those you perceive as not doing their fair share. You are also stubborn and are highly sensitive to negative thoughts around you. You can't tolerate strife and confusion, and you don't take nonsense from anyone. Your biggest challenge is to look into the deeper meaning of life's experiences.

Best Trait: Everyone admires your sense of fair play.

Your Space: You love your backyard and have done a great job of caring for it. Inside, you prefer traditional dark woods, a well-appointed dining room, and unusual items, often antiques like a wonderful grandfather clock. You also enjoy your herb garden.

Career: Because you wholly dedicate yourself to whatever you do, you're exceptionally capable in careers that require you to put in a lot of time and effort, such as politics, health care, and teaching. You might also excel in any career that provides an outlet for your self-expression. Of course, the traditional occupation for you would be a parson, as was the original John Russell, but parsons are scarce these days.

Your Inner Dog

Leisure Time and Entertainment: You like to watch television sitcoms, especially endless *Frasier* reruns; you really like Eddie. (His real name was Moose.) You just can't get enough of sitcoms and end up laughing and laughing. (No one is around while you do this, of course.) For books and movies, anything about vampires strikes your fancy. You like to read philosophical works as well, especially a nice volume of Saint Thomas Aquinas, before you go to bed. You are also athletic and enjoy competitive games that call for bursts of speed. (In school, you excelled at relay races.)

If you decide to go abroad, a trip back to your pet's Devonshire, England, homeland would be lovely. You also like places where you can just have a good time—one reason that you enjoy cruises where you can indulge your every whim.

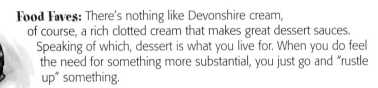

Fashion Musts: You look great in chic, modern clothing that features bold colors and patterns. For a night out with friends or a special someone, try a cocktail dress by Narciso Rodriguez—his line features clean silhouettes and feminine detailing that will flatter your figure. Consider adding a pair of leopard heels to really get people talking! Your jewelry is simple but usually expensive.

Food Faves: There's nothing like Devonshire cream, of course, a rich clotted cream that makes great dessert sauces. Speaking of which, dessert is what you live for. When you do feel the need for something more substantial, you just go and "rustle up" something.

Significant Others: You prefer to date a variety of people, and you usually don't like to feel tied down. Once you fall seriously in love, though, it is indeed serious. You do best with someone who can inspire you to be your best, someone who is strong willed, steady, and persistent. Stay away from people with a brooding, sulky temperament.

Other Compatible Breed Personalities: Besides the Jack Russell Terrier, you are compatible with Borzoi and Brussels Griffons.

Pet Peeve: You hate it when people shirk responsibility.

Lucky Number: Numerological calculations for your breed reveal your lucky number to be 8.

Notable Jack Russell People: Sandra Bullock, Mariah Carey, Audrey Hepburn, Bette Midler

Personality and Character: The Lhasa Apso owner has one of the most complex personalities of all dog owners, and in fact you are sometimes conflicted. On one hand, you are an imaginative, lively, and cheerful person, esteemed by all. Indeed, Lhasa people have a large and devoted circle of friends. You have a truly joyful attitude toward life. You are utterly fearless and willing to take on responsibility. You are neither a follower nor a leader—you do your own thing and have a deep-in-the-bone flinty resolution about you. At the same time, you have a good-natured live-and-let-live attitude (necessary when owning a Lhasa). Most of the time, you live by the Golden Rule, which is one reason why you have so many friends. You are able to delay gratification and deal with frustration in an admirable manner. You are also a true original, full of creative ideas, and a risk taker. You value knowledge intensely and crave intellectual stimulation. Yet . . . you have a dark side. You can be deeply sad and worry over nothing. Sometimes you find it hard to make a simple decision and to set goals, and you can be dreamy and vague. And perhaps most troubling of all, you are not very good at taking phone messages and passing them along. You are, however, very good at getting to places and appointments on time, and that's pretty important.

Best Traits: You are original and possess a willingness to take risks.

Your Space: The most important room in your house is the kitchen—you certainly spend a lot of time there. However, unlike most people, it's done in cool rather than warm colors. Your furniture is often avant-garde.

Your Inner Dog

Career: You would excel as an occupational therapist, social psychologist, or realtor. When at work, you need to isolate yourself from outside noises.

Leisure Time and Entertainment: You love ancient literature, especially works by Homer. You know that literature reached its peak with its first great books—why bother to read further? As far as music is concerned, you like classic rock like The Who and Led Zeppelin. For sports, it's baseball during the season and poker the rest of the time. You also enjoy practicing the martial arts and playing tennis.

When it comes to vacation, you have a wanderlust and a passion for the mountains, the mountains, and the mountains again. Consider visiting the Himalayas!

Fashion Musts: When you're feeling down, a new purse or pair of shoes often puts things into perspective. You like interesting, avant-garde fashion, like that designed by Alexander McQueen.

Food Faves: Cheeseburgers, roast lamb, and moussaka are favorites. You love to go out to dinner. Real Tibetan tea, the kind with yak butter in it, leaves you unmoved—even if that's what they drink in Tibet, your Lhaso's homeland. Sometimes you can only go so far in honor of your dog.

Significant Others: You are a true romantic, loving and warmhearted, and can draw out the mystical dimension in all relationships. However, because you are exceptionally forceful and intelligent, you run the risk of being a dictator in any relationship. You become extremely attached to one person, often to the point of not letting them have any privacy—it's something you have to watch.

Compatible Animals: Besides Lhasas, you are compatible with Chinese Cresteds and designer dogs.

Pet Peeve: You're not a fan of beauty contests.

Notable Lhasa Apso People: Dalai Lama, Jodie Sweetin, Kerry Washington

Personality and Character: If you've got it, flaunt it! You Poodle people just sparkle. You are proud, graceful, and never lacking in self-esteem. You're also known for your manners—you always recognize what fork to use and that sort of thing. You tend to talk a lot; however, what you say is so interesting that you usually keep the attention of others, even when you are giving orders (which is often). Some people may find you "hard to take," possibly because they can't live up to your standards. Detractors may call you "elitist," but it's more accurate to say that you are discriminating. You compete in everything from beauty pageants to ballroom dance and usually win. You are extremely sensitive, so much so that you can become ill when overstressed. You thrive best in a peaceful environment and do not tolerate loud, argumentative people.

Best Trait: Your social intelligence is your best trait.

Your Space: Your favorite room is your bedroom—after all, this is where you get your beauty rest, and it's also where you indulge your most imaginative fancies. In fact, your bedroom resembles a first-class hotel room. Your criteria for a perfect room go beyond painting the walls pink; you require great acoustics, excellent ventilation, and super insulation. Poodle people often insist on walk-in closets with lights that turn on automatically when the door is opened and a dimmer control on everything.

Career: Oh, the arts—or politics! While you can find Poodle people in many professions, you are born to be center stage. You would also do well in any career that requires you to speak French.

Leisure Time and Entertainment: You may look like a fashion plate, but Poodle people make surprisingly good athletes. You may not be much of a swimmer (too much trouble redoing your hair), but you love splashing in the water. In fact, it's fair to say that you make a splash wherever you go. You tend to participate in sports that have the most à la mode outfits. That's why you like ice skating—you can really indulge in all that glitter. You also love reading Miss Manners (for her taste), Jane Austen (for her charm), and *Le Monde* (to practice your French). When it comes to literature, you are quite fond of that man of the world Henry James, even if the Poodle in *Roderick Hudson* is rather a villain—or at least belongs to one.

Your favorite vacation destinations involve a day at the beach and a night on the town. The best beaches are on the Riviera, of course. With its thriving nightlife, Buenos Aires may also be a good place for you to visit.

Fashion Musts: Your best physical feature is your remarkable hair, which, once you learn to tame it, proves a wonderful instrument for self-expression. If you're an athlete, keep it short and chic—its natural body will get you through an Ironman triathlon. You appear at your best in high heels and a glamorous gown (especially if it's a Christian Lacroix!), but you surprise everyone on Saturday morning at the gym or jogging club with that glittery sweat suit. (Your friends laugh until they see you work out.) You also shine in lots of jewelry, and you can make rhinestones look like diamonds. Above all else, resist the urge to wear a poodle skirt, although it's okay to paint your toenails pink.

Food Faves: You love gourmet foods like caviar, foie gras, and truffles. You can eat rich food without gaining an inch or a pound, although you do watch your portions.

Significant Others: Poodle people require a calm and motivated partner—someone who appreciates your special qualities. You also need someone as versatile as you are. Stay away from those self-centered types. A mate who doesn't mind taking a back seat to you may be especially compatible.

Other Compatible Breed Personalities: Besides the Poodle, you are compatible with Cocker Spaniels and Shar-Peis.

Pet Peeve: Your biggest pet peeve is people who misunderstand Poodles—they just don't get it.

Lucky Number: Numerological calculations for your breed reveal your lucky number to be 3 if you have a Standard Poodle, 6 for a Miniature, and 1 for a Toy.

Notable Poodle People: Joan Crawford, Walt Disney, Katharine Hepburn, Jack Lemmon, John Steinbeck

Smart and Sassy

Personality and Character: You have extraordinary gifts in many areas, from art to science. You feel a strong need to express yourself in your own distinctive, individual way. Friendly and soft-hearted, you would never knowingly hurt another person or animal. However, you are not afraid of what anyone else thinks, and this allows you to live your life the way you want to. You are extremely conscientious and interested in serving humanity, and you have strong networking skills. You enjoy people and are stimulating, highly entertaining company. You are always ready to acknowledge your failures and accept constructive criticism. You are a sucker for compliments and can be quite gullible—it is sometimes difficult for you to distinguish between what is true and false.

Best Trait: Your conscientiousness is your best trait.

Your Space: You enjoy a cozy, secure home that gives the appearance of having a thatched roof, even if it doesn't. Your favorite room is your den, where you can enjoy a mini retirement from the world. Even highly social Sheltie people need a few moments to themselves. You are especially found of traditional low-seated driftwood Shetland chairs. (There are almost no trees on the Shetland islands.)

Career: Anything in the hospitality or craft fields would be suitable for you because you excel at entertaining and enjoy things like baking, cooking, knitting, and sewing.

Leisure Time and Entertainment: You enjoy doing all sorts of arts and crafts, especially with textiles. Many Sheltie people are excellent potters as well. For exercise, a simple walk in the country suits you just fine—you're not too fond of organized sports or competitive activities.

When it comes to vacation, you dream of faraway places, although you like to vacation close to home best of all. You also might want to consider visiting the Shetland Islands, the original home of your breed.

Fashion Musts: You are fond of knitwear and leather—handcrafted in Shetland, if possible. Simple sportswear is also a favorite—Givenchy makes some great pieces with interesting detailing. Jazz up your outfit with some jewelry— maybe a strand of pearls. This will keep you soft and romantic even with your tennis shoes and comfortable clothing.

Food Faves: Anything with chocolate pleases your palate (with the exception of chocolate-covered insects). You are also addicted to your morning bowl of cereal, with skim milk, of course. And as a tribute to the Shetland isles, you will eat smoked salmon, smoked mackerel, and kippers, even if no one else will.

Significant Others: You have the rare ability to direct your affections, which means that you are not a victim of love but its master. Your unique combination of firmness and flexibility makes you easy to love—and makes it easy for you to love others. You also have great intuition when it comes to choosing the right mate. Overall, you will fare best with someone who appreciates hearth and home, much like yourself.

Other Compatible Breed Personalities: Besides the Sheltie, you are compatible with Airedale Terriers and Finnish Spitzes.

Pet Peeve: You hate rain, especially when it's accompanied by lightning.

Lucky Number: Numerological calculations for your breed reveal your lucky number to be 9.

Notable Sheltie People: Calvin Coolidge

Personality and Character: You know exactly who you are and what your purpose is in life. Outspoken, high minded, and assertive, you are a noble seeker of truth and can see many sides of an argument. You prefer to act immediately rather than sitting around weighing options endlessly, opting for risk over security. You also love speed, adventure, and freedom, and you rely on improvisation rather than planning. You long for change and excitement and want to take an active part in life. Impatient by nature, you are more driven than most people, and you are loyal to your teammates. But it's your leadership skills, motivation, and hardworking nature that really push you to the head of the pack. Because of your charm, it is easy for you to make new friends, and because of your nobility and strength, you are able to keep them. (You are also very protective of them.) You tend to scatter your energy in all different directions, so learn what it is that will give you the balance and "connectiveness" that you require.

Best Trait: You are a wonderful leader, and a lot of people look up to you because of it.

Your Space: You love the great outdoors, no matter the weather, although you are frankly not crazy about heat and humidity. You'd rather live in an igloo. Your home is a nurturing place that provides the comfort and relaxation you need in your busy life.

Career: You have the drive to succeed and would excel in a leadership role in a variety of careers, especially politics and entrepreneurial business adventures.

Leisure Time and Entertainment: You are a sports lover, and you enjoy working out at the gym and power walking several times a week. Of course, you also have a fondness for adventure stories, especially those by Jack London. For music, you like songs that are up-tempo and powerful—nothing soft or sentimental.

When you go on vacation, your goal is to get away from it all. You prefer the mountains to the beach and the north to the south. Siberia isn't totally out of the question, either—it would be a great adventure.

Fashion Musts: You find traditional Siberian fashion to be quite lovely, especially the brocaded fabrics and quilted coats. When it comes to your everyday style, though, you prefer flowing, feminine pieces with a gypsy-like vibe—especially dresses by designer Nanette Lepore, which feature lively, colorful prints.

Food Faves: Classics like cheeseburgers, french fries, and cupcakes are some of your favorites. You also like to try some traditional Siberian foods, such as *okroshka* (salad made from radishes, onions, cucumbers, and eggs, dressed with *kvas*—a mildly alcoholic drink made from rye), *gruzdianka* (milk and mushroom stew), and *pelmeni* (dumplings with meat filling).

Significant Others: When it comes to romance, you are the sentimental type, but in the long run, you'll be happiest with someone who is a stabilizing, loyal influence. You are charmingly not possessive, and this makes you even more attractive.

Other Compatible Breed Personalities: Besides the Siberian Husky, you are compatible with Boxers and Weimaraners.

Pet Peeve: Whiny children are your biggest pet peeve.

Lucky Number: Numerological calculations for your breed reveal your lucky number to be 8.

Notable Siberian Husky People: Louis Koo Tin Lok, Ronald Reagan

Personality and Character: You are amiable, sensitive, and friendly, but you also have a great intensity about you. You will do anything for success. You love to take a gamble, and Whippet people often walk that fine line between success and failure. Other people often respond to your slightest suggestions, for you have a strong creative streak especially appreciated by your superiors. (However, it's sometimes too easy for you to promise to get something done before a certain date, even though you know in your heart of hearts that's it's just not going to happen.) You sometimes have trouble expressing your feelings directly, and you change your mind quite often. In some cases, you may find it necessary to compromise (and develop a slightly thicker skin) to gain your goals.

Best Trait: You have the ability to nurture plants, animals, and people.

Your Space: You need a positive physical environment in which you can grow spiritually. With your home decor, you are drawn to bright, cheerful colors like yellow, but you also appreciate light greens and blues for a more relaxing touch. Your favorite room is the kitchen, where you can express both your warmth and your creativity. You enjoy looking for ways to make spaces serve more than one purpose, and your home always features the newest electronics.

Your Inner Dog

Career: Because of your creative nature, you would do well in a career in the arts, but you can handle almost any kind of job and be equally happy.

Leisure Time and Entertainment: When it comes to music, you love classic rock like The Who and the Beatles. (Try as you might, you can't quite get into Guiding Voices' *The Pipe Dreams of Instant Prince Whippet*, even if the album does feature the name of your dog.) You're also a huge fan of Agatha Christie mysteries and Wallace and Gromit's *The Whippet Vanishes*. You enjoy yoga as well and are one of the few people who can manage the lotus position.

For vacation—to sunny Spain! You like the Caribbean islands, too. Sunny locales and their attendant warmth deeply appeal to your own warm and sensitive nature. Like your dog, you just can't bear the cold.

Fashion Musts: You have one of those enviable figures that couture clothes were just made for—and your artistic side really appreciates fashion as high art. Designer Marc Bouwer makes some of your favorite evening gowns, with their extremely detailed beadwork and sleek silhouettes.

Food Faves: For Whippet owners, there's nothing that beats whipped cream and anything that goes with it—especially strawberries, gingerbread, cobblers, and sundaes. You also love a good milkshake. You are much more of a nibbler than one to tuck into a heavy sit-down meal, and your entrees are often vegetarian. You especially love healthy salads. That way, you can save room for dessert. You have to maintain your elegant figure somehow!

Significant Others: You're attracted to anyone with an accent, but that's as far as your snobbery goes. You would get along best with someone quiet, undemanding, and unobtrusive. If you select someone as emotionally sensitive as you are, it could be a difficult relationship.

Other Compatible Breed Personalities: Besides the Whippet, you are compatible with Border Collies and Maltese.

Pet Peeve: It bothers you when people don't put things back where they belong—especially *your* things.

Lucky Number: Numerological calculations for your breed reveal your lucky number to be 7.

Notable Whippet People: Julian Clary

Chapter 5
Cultured and Classic

Afghan Hound People • Basset Hound People • Bernese Mountain Dog People • Bloodhound People • Boston Terrier People • Cocker Spaniel People • Dalmatian People • Great Dane People • Irish Setter People • Neapolitan Mastiff People • Newfoundland People • Old English Sheepdog People • Saluki People • Weimaraner People • Vizsla People

Personality and Character: You are a wholesome person with an unmistakable air of quiet dignity, seriousness, and even aloofness. At the same time, you are extremely energetic and competitive. You have a great deal of inner strength and are able to focus your energies to overcome hardship. You are also much more interested in thinking for yourself than in following someone else's directives, and at times, you are not as "precise" about details as some would wish. When it comes to trivia, though, you know your stuff! (You're one of those rather annoying people who know all 2,364 uses for baking soda and insist on telling people about them.)

Best Trait: Your resilience is quite admirable.

Your Space: You have a fondness for high altitudes, and you're happy in a tent, recalling your dog's ancient days among the Bedouins. Your favorite room is your bedroom, where you can indulge without shame your love for afghans, which you make yourself, turning a sleeping room into a true living room. You do some of your most important planning here. You also have a green thumb that is the envy of the neighborhood—you could make a desert bloom.

Career: You would be a terrific in a career in which you can be self-employed, such as a life coach or artist. A bit of a nomad, you like to switch positions within your career field, which keeps things interesting. You have a strong personal commitment to your work—it is never just a job.

Leisure Time and Entertainment: Your favorite books include *The Afghan* by Frederick Forsyth (a spy thriller), as well as *The Kite Runner* and *A Thousand Splendid Suns* by Khaled Hosseini. Not only do these works give you important insights about the land of your dog's birth, but they also appeal to your serious side. You can also quote poetry by the hour. Modern art is your favorite, particularly that of Pablo Picasso, a fellow Afghan owner—you love his cubist paintings. And of course you enjoy knitting and crocheting for a quiet evening at home. For sports, you favor soccer—not as an observer but as a strong and vigorous player. If you can't play a sport, in fact, you don't have much interest in it.

Your ideal vacation involves open spaces, mountains, and solitary time. You might even enjoy combining a vacation with gem hunting or panning for gold—this will get you outside communing with nature, and you might strike it rich, too. North Carolina, Nevada, and California are wonderful treasure-hunting packages!

Fashion Musts: Your personal style tends toward a more basic aesthetic, but you love to make a statement with your accessories. Whether it's a scarf, shoe, or great piece of jewelry, you're always on the lookout for something new and exciting. Try a Gucci ornamental studded belt or printed bag to complement your look.

Food Faves: You enjoy sampling Afghan classics like lamb with spinach, meatballs with noodles tossed in yogurt, and chicken and chickpea stew. Tea is usually your beverage of choice. You are certainly not one for junk food—you'd much prefer to look up interesting and new recipes. It should be said, though, that sometimes you prefer that other people actually cook them.

Significant Others: When it comes to relationships, you have deep feelings. Look for someone who is not overly materialistic or impulsive. However, don't be afraid to embrace your fantasies— they can come true. Your best partner is an intriguing, otherworldly person who holds the same values and ideals that you do. You tend to make the best romantic connections when you are involved in a team or community effort.

Other Compatible Breed Personalities: Besides the Afghan Hound, you are compatible with Chihuahuas and Pekingese.

Pet Peeve: It drives you crazy when people cannot follow simple directions—your directions, that is.

Lucky Number: Numerological calculations for your breed reveal your lucky number to be 9.

Notable Afghan Hound People: Gary Cooper, Pablo Picasso

Cultured and Classic

Personality and Character: You are a truly original character who prefers to experiment rather than follow tradition.

People consider you enigmatic, perhaps even obscure. You care about fair play, integrity, and harmony, although sometimes you fight with others for a position on center stage. You love to laugh but not at others; in fact, you are in tune with the sufferings of others and are perceptive of their feelings. You are interested in helping them, and you benefit from contact with lots of people. You have a rich and exciting dream life, but too much activity in real life can get on your nerves. You work with great dedication toward your goals, but sometimes you let criticism get the best of you. Don't give in to doubt, and don't be afraid to seek guidance when you really need it.

Best Trait: You live in accordance with your inner values.

Your Space: Your study is your favorite space because it is your retreat against the world. And even though you tend to complain about it (a lot), you actually rather enjoy doing things around the house. Basset Hound owners often like abstract art and quirky pieces of furniture.

Career: Basset Hound owners do well when they are self-employed. A career as a writer, for example, would suit you well. Basset people are also found in large numbers in the helping professions, especially as doctors and teachers. They also often work for causes such as environmental protection and animal welfare.

Your Inner Dog

Leisure Time and Entertainment: You have a wonderful singing voice. You also enjoy good literature, especially poetry in the form of sonnets and haiku. And of course, there's Homer's *Odyssey*—it reminds you of all the times you have had to wander around yourself, looking for your dog. For a less strenuous evening, you go for pulp fiction and the comics. You also like taking long walks, either alone or with a significant other, but you're always happiest if your Basset can come along as well. You enjoy many kinds of music, but frankly, nothing suits you as well as the sweet sound of your own dog howling at the moon—or more likely, at nothing at all.

For vacation, consider the French countryside, where you can connect with your breed's roots. Basset owners also have a passionate desire to gather together with other Basset owners in massive packs called "waddles," which can be found in California, Michigan, Maryland, and New Jersey.

Fashion Musts: You love timeless jerseys and shift dresses or A-line skirts (perfect for flattering almost any figure). Designer Derek Lam's signature feminine pieces with their clean, tailored silhouettes would suit your style well. Watch your accessories, though—they should add to, not detract from, your overall look.

Food Faves: Basset owners are fond of food, just like their dogs, and have an untidy tendency to share their meals with their dogs. As a result, Basset owners often choose to eat dog-friendly items, like hamburgers with everything on them. Your favorite desserts include apple pie (with or without mom), and at Easter, you must have your chocolate bunnies. (Those are the one thing your dog doesn't get to share.)

Significant Others: You need someone who is strong and able, and Basset Hound owners are famous for establishing long, successful relationships. You have an unqualified commitment to the partner of your choice. You love your mate more and more with every passing year. Of course, you'll probably fall in love with another Basset Hound owner!

Other Compatible Breed Personalities: Besides the Basset Hound, you are compatible with Bloodhounds and Old English Sheepdogs.

Pet Peeve: You hate it when people criticize you.

Lucky Number: Numerological calculations for your breed reveal your lucky number to be 2.

Notable Basset Hound People: Clint Eastwood, Bob Hope

Cultured and Classic

Personality and Character: You are a self-confident person with broad intellectual interests and a judicious turn of mind. You do kind things for others not because you have to but because you want to. You also enjoy giving gifts, especially things that you have baked or crafted. At the same time, you enjoy buying things for yourself (which sometimes cost a lot more than you are willing to admit). You are a patient, responsive, and attentive listener, and you don't mind letting others have the spotlight—you're content to watch from the wings. Sometimes you have trouble letting go of the past, and you can become overly nostalgic. (You'll always wish you were 25 again!)

Best Trait: Your good nature is your best trait.

Your Space: A Swiss chalet is your dream home, although you're quite happy in the home you have. Your decor is simple, traditional, and uncomplicated and is based first and foremost on comfort. Your favorite room in your home is the bedroom, and you do like your sleep! It can get a little messy, though, if you don't keep on top of it. Your home is always one of the first in the neighborhood to feature festive outdoor holiday decorations. Some people (and the dog) complain that you keep the house too warm, but that's the way you like it.

Career: You believe in yourself, and it's important for you to choose a career in which you can climb to the top without being "bossy." You would do well in higher education, especially in the humanities, where you can combine your intellectual interests. You might also do well in the travel industry, planning vacations for others.

　　　　　　Your Inner Dog

Leisure Time and Entertainment: One of your favorite leisure activities is talking on the phone. You are also a lover of the arts, the blues, basket weaving, starry nights, and bungee jumping. Superman is your favorite heroic character. He reminds you of yourself in so many ways, as you too hide your own fabulous and heroic qualities until the time is right to unveil them. Charlotte Brontë is your favorite writer, and you must have read *Jane Eyre* ten times—she appeals to the wild romance in your heart. But nothing beats the Sherlock Holmes stories, some of which take place at Reichenbach Falls in the heart of the Berner Oberland, the home of your breed.

For vacation, try traveling by train to the Jungfraujoch in Switzerland, which is in the heart of the Berner Oberland. The train takes you right up to the yoke of the Eiger and Jungfrau—the views are fabulous—and you can ski and get a suntan at the same time. Be sure to go when the sun is shining! Don't miss Interlaken, either.

Fashion Musts: You look great in smooth, soft fabrics and value comfort in your everyday wear. In fact, if you can get away with it, a simple cotton T-shirt and a well-worn pair of jeans are your daily uniform. When you have an event to attend, however, you know how to bring in the glamour while still keeping your look understated—a Vera Wang gown would be perfect for those special occasions.

Food Faves: You enjoy an eclectic choice of foods, favoring a combination of German and northern Italian dishes, both of which are common in the Berner Oberland. But casual dining is a must. You'd prefer not dining out if you have to wear anything fancier than a sweater.

Significant Others: While you are able to make a strong commitment (and are secure in your relationship), you do fantasize from time to time about lost chances and unavailable celebrities. However, you wouldn't attempt to put those fantasies into action. You are not one who is always trying to change or gain power over the other person. You are a caring, kindhearted, doting, and attentive mate. However, if you are badly treated, you are not above taking a very effective revenge.

Other Compatible Breed Personalities: Besides the Bernese Mountain Dog, you are compatible with Pugs and Scottish Terriers.

Pet Peeve: You dislike having to witness other people's dramatic "scenes."

Lucky Number: Numerological calculations for your breed reveal your lucky number to be 3.

Notable Bernese People: Goldie Hawn, Robert Redford

Cultured and Classic

Personality and Character: Bloodhound people tend to be original thinkers who are strongly self-reliant, compelling, loyal, and confident. (You'd be a good candidate for *Survivor*, in fact.) You love to learn, but you are happiest when you can apply your knowledge practically. You are inexhaustibly thorough and determined. At the same time, you are open-minded and flexible about how you get things done, very open to new ideas and new experiences. You are also a natural diplomat who can use persuasion rather than threats or force to get what you want done. In other words, you have great social intelligence. You tend to be quiet and somewhat shy; you don't like large gatherings and noisy parties. You can also get lost in your own secret world. You are not very adept at planning ahead. Although you have traditional values, you tend to ignore legal and even moral codes when they get in your way. You are closely in touch with your feelings, and you are rarely depressed. Intuitive to the extreme, you like to "follow your nose," so to speak, wherever it leads—which can sometimes be into trouble. If there is something hidden, you and only you will find it. (You and your dog claim to be the only ones who know where Jimmy Hoffa really is.)

Best Trait: You are able to finish what you—or other people—start.

Your Space: Your garden is your world. It should be filled with the rich fragrances you and your Bloodhound crave: lilacs, hyacinths, viburnum, and above all, the legendary scent of daphne. You also enjoy the subtler scents of apple and pear blossoms. As for the inside of your home, you don't really care how its decorated—you are way more of an outdoorsy kind of person.

Your Inner Dog

Career: Bloodhound people make great detectives and law enforcement officials—your intuition is rarely faulty.

Leisure Time and Entertainment: You like hiking and jogging (and have participated in a marathon or two). When it's too nasty to go out, nothing suits you like a game of bridge—your intuition makes you a winner every time. One of your favorite artists is John Sargent Noble, who painted the beautiful Bloodhound portrait *On Scent*. You like reading the works of philosophers and theologians like Thomas Aquinas and Augustine, as it suits your skilled, relentless mind. However, you are distressed by *The Hound of the Baskervilles*—Bloodhounds are never as ferocious as the one portrayed in the book.

When it comes to vacation, try Corfu, Greece, Croatia, or Germany. You are the one who enjoys the out-of-the way treasures these places can provide. Only you can nose them out.

Fashion Musts: For everyday, you like to dress casually—you feel best in a simple cotton T-shirt. You look great in plaids—and a trench coat. That should go without saying. You love Lacoste's tailored, preppy sportswear.

Food Faves: You enjoy eating very much and like simple, classic foods like oatmeal, bologna sandwiches, hamburgers, and apple pie. You can smell food a mile away.

Significant Others: You are extremely affectionate and enjoy the company of someone rather old-fashioned, who enjoys going for long, quiet walks and prefers letter writing to e-mail. And you want someone who will age well because you plan on being together forever. You'd also like to find someone who is a good cook; that's pretty important, too.

Other Compatible Breed Personalities: Besides the Bloodhound, you are compatible with American Staffordshire Terriers and Great Danes.

Pet Peeve: Leftovers—you give them to the dog.

Lucky Number: Numerological calculations for your breed eveal your lucky number to be 2.

Notable Bloodhound People: Charles Dickens, Sir Walter Scott, Queen Victoria of England

Cultured and Classic

Boston Terrier People

Personality and Character: You are not only sophisticated but a serious thinker with plenty of common sense, too. You have a broad range of interests and are a true diplomat. You also possess a high level of social intelligence and manage to fit in anywhere. Although you are a little shy and slow to trust others, you are well liked and easy to be around. Organized and intense, you can handle stress better than most, and you're not in danger of being overemotional (although your emotions may be stronger than you like to admit). You are slightly self-centered but responsible (and a reliable secret keeper). You are one of the few who can turn a theory into action, and you are not afraid to take a stand, even in the face of strong opposition. Pain and disappointment sometimes get the better of you, but most of the time you are silent and strong, even in the face of great adversity. You are sympathetic, congenial, and considerate—a true nurturer and protector.

Best Trait: You have a tremendously civilizing influence upon others—even your handwriting is a model of elegance.

Your Space: Your favorite outdoor space is Fenway Park, which is one of the oldest baseball parks still in use. After all, if a Boston Terrier is not a cosmopolitan dog, who is? Obsessively neat, you like to spend your spare time organizing the garage. As for the rest of the house, the kitchen is the hub of action. It's a big one, with all new appliances. You decorate with soft, subtle colors.

Career Opportunities: Consider the entertainment industry or a position as a corporate executive—or any position in which you can combine your ability to deal with others while exercising your excellent organizational abilities. The stressful worlds of entertainment and big business bother you not in the least—you thrive in them.

Leisure Time and Entertainment: Taking it easy is one of your favorite things to do. You are interested in Chinese philosophers such as Confucius and Lao-Tzu, but you have also made a study of Japan's Bushid code of conduct, the code of Samurai warriors. Another favorite hobby is watching shows on television, like *Boston Legal*. You are a world traveler and want to visit a new country every year. But there's nothing like a great game with the Red Sox, Patriots, or Celtics for real enjoyment.

Fashion Musts: Everyone knows your style: exquisitely tailored and quietly sophisticated pastels, like dusty rose, and dainty jewelry. Your biggest fashion mistake is trying to change your hair color too frequently. One of your favorite designers is Ralph Lauren, that quintessential American designer.

Food Faves: Boston cream pie, Boston cod, blueberry muffins, scrod, roast beef (rare), and baked beans. You also like mincemeat pies, but at least you don't inflict your unusual preference on others. You like to drink tea and especially enjoy tea parties. You also like to cook, especially for your family.

Significant Others: You strongly enjoy the attentions of potential suitors and love to flirt. In fact, your flirtatious nature can get you into trouble with your significant other. Your main problems are that you can sometimes become distracted and unavailable.

Compatible Dogs: Besides the Boston Terrier, you are compatible with Chow Chows and Miniature Pinschers.

Pet Peeve: Pushy Christmas shoppers are your biggest pet peeve.

Lucky Number: Numerological calculations for your breed reveal your lucky number to be 7.

Notable Boston Terrier People: Yasmine Bleeth, Famke Janssen, Denise Richards, Joan Rivers

Personality and Character: You are a hard worker with tremendous endurance, and you are known for your inner strength and courage. You hold yourself to high standards and are tremendously capable of organizing and running things. Never would you let fear or pain stand in the way of what you want. On occasion, however, you have been known to take on more than you can do reasonably well, and when you meet with success in one field, you are likely to walk away and try another. Curiously, despite your passion for work, materialism and money are not at the top of your agenda. You have the charming notion that good will always triumph over evil. Your sense of diplomacy helps you achieve your goals, and you see everything from the human angle. You have a strong appreciation for beauty, as well as an innate charm and humor.

Best Trait: You have acquired the art of happiness, and that is no small thing.

Your Space: A Spanish hacienda is definitely you—one with a big, spacious kitchen, the hub of the house, and the place from which you reign. Yours is filled with color and traditional decorative arts, as well as pottery and dishware. You want everything just so and do everything you can to make it that way. However, considering your passion for cleanliness and your persnicketyness about your laundry, it might be wise to hire some help.

Career: Look for a career in the arts or engineering, where you can exercise your passion for exactness and beauty. You are especially

Your Inner Dog

attracted to working on large, complex projects that are well beyond the grasp of other people. Whatever you do, make sure that you're well paid—you're worth it!

Leisure Time and Entertainment: Sometimes you just like to shut down and enjoy old Shirley Temple movies. In the afternoon it's Oprah, who, like you, is a lover of Cockers. You also like artwork that features your favorite breed, such as contemporary artist Roy Andersen's Cocker Spaniel portraits. It may seem a cliché, but you love rock and blues and have an especial fondness for the power and strength of Joe Cocker's music (the early stuff, of course). You're not much of a fiction reader—when you pick up a book, it's usually factual or a how-to manual. When you relax, you relax as completely as you work and are likely to sink into a comfortable chair and just doze. Only it's more like a power nap—when you wake up, you are ready to tackle the next big project.

For vacation, consider taking a trip to Spain, the original home of the Cocker Spaniel. In general, though, you are fonder of shorter trips around your home—it doesn't do to be away for too long. Whenever you leave the house, your computer, planner, and cell phone go with you.

Fashion Musts: You have a regal air about you, and you love dramatic evening wear that makes you feel like a princess. In fact, dressing up is second nature to you, and you have impeccable taste. For a classic, romantic look, try a gown by designer Reem Acra. When it comes to your hair, simple is often quite flattering and easier to deal with. (After all, it's hard enough to keep up with your Cocker's 'do!)

Food Faves: You enjoy elegant Spanish food and like to experiment with various forms of paella (Spanish stew flavored with chicken, rice, and more than a hint of saffron), tortillas, flan (custard with a caramel glaze), and gazpachos (a spicy soup served cold). Actually, all this cooking gives you more time to enjoy your big kitchen and use those fancy plates.

Significant Others: You are very loyal and capable of deep feelings, but you can be a serious flirt, too. It is imperative for you to find a suitable life partner for your happiness. You lavish your family and loved ones with everything they desire, and you are well suited to domestic life.

Other Compatible Breed Personalities: Besides the Cocker Spaniel, you are compatible with Poodles and Shar-Peis.

Pet Peeve: You hate it when people have bad table manners—especially when they chew with their mouth open.

Lucky Number: Numerological calculations for your breed reveal your lucky number to be 5.

Notable Cocker Spaniel People: Bill Clinton, Sugar Ray Leonard, Steven Spielberg, Charlize Theron, Oprah Winfrey

Dalmatian People

Personality and Character: You have a well-developed sense of who you are and where you are in the world. You are a gripping conversationalist: focused, enthusiastic, and a good listener. You can grace any social situation with your inborn courtesy, entertaining ways, and quiet amiability. Partnership and team efforts are really important to you, but let's face it—you love the spotlight! (Is this why you have a spotted dog?) You are highly sociable but capable of great austerity when needed. You are also flexible and open-minded, very effective in dealing with people and always willing to consider different viewpoints. You have never lacked a purpose in life, but sometimes you may seem to have too many purposes! You are easily bored by the tedium of everyday life and seek to transcend it. You have also been known to distort facts, just the tiniest bit; perhaps you have a somewhat unreliable memory. In addition, some Dal people are tremendous procrastinators.

Best Trait: You are extremely empathetic, and your family and friends know that they can always count on you to be a good listener.

Your Space: You like any place that is candlelit. Unfortunately, your housekeeping can be a little spotty, so the darker the better. Your favorite room in your home is the living room, but it is so much more. You can transform your traditional formal living room space into a multipurpose area. Consider adding a fireplace and plenty of bookshelves. (You are an inveterate reader—better go floor to ceiling.) A couple of overstuffed chairs, a sofa, and a table for homework or art projects complete the picture.

Your Inner Dog

Career: Look for a career in social work, filmmaking, or a technical field, and look for one with plenty of challenges. You find routine work somewhat tedious and should not be trapped behind a desk all day. Don't forget firefighting, if you wish to be conventional, although it has to be said that most Dalmatian owners aren't firefighters.

Leisure Time and Entertainment: You love to read and especially enjoy plays, from dramas like *King Lear* to tragedies like *The Oresteia*, because of their passion and deep knowledge of the human condition. You also love the works of the American tragic playwright Eugene O'Neill, a fellow Dalmatian owner. You enjoy reading autobiographies as well. You love art that features your breed, like the portraits by American artist Gustav Muss-Arnolt. And of course, you have a passion for fire trucks. One of your favorite movies is the classic *101 Dalmatians* but only for sentimental reasons.

For vacation, it's off to the beautiful Dalmatian coast. It is, as you know, the next Riviera. It has not only the most stunning landscape in Europe but an exciting nightlife—and just as important, it won't break your bank account. For a side trip, consider visiting nearby Greece and Croatia.

Fashion Musts: You like chic, well-made clothing that accentuates your figure without overwhelming it, and you gravitate toward designers like Carolina Herrera who know how to make sophisticated yet ready-to-wear pieces. Black and white are your signature colors, of course, but whatever you do, stay away from polka dots!

Food Faves: You love the foods of your dog's native Dalmatia: olives and olive oils, vinegars, capers, fig preserves, spices, sauces, and Croatian wine. Then there's that famous Dalmatian fish soup. Lamb is your meat of choice. And you can't get started without your morning cup of coffee.

Significant Others: Love and marriage are important to you, and you are automatically drawn to good spouse material: someone who's loving, sincere, and has a sense of humor. You do best with someone who is strong but not overbearing. Your affections are deep, fixed, and unpretending, yet when times are bad, you can detach emotionally and withdraw. In general, Dalmatian people have very happy marriages and partnerships.

Other Compatible Breed Personalities: Besides the Dalmatian, you are compatible with Dachshunds and Portuguese Water Dogs.

Pet Peeve: You hate receiving solicitation calls at home.

Lucky Number: Numerological calculations for your breed reveal your lucky number to be 3.

Notable Dalmatian People: Dick Clark, Gloria Estefan, Michael J. Fox, Rock Hudson, Eugene O'Neill

Great Dane People

Personality and Character: Dedicated and ambitious, you're always striving to make your life better—you like to think of it as a masterpiece in progress. Even though you often prefer not to be the leader, you perform extremely well in supportive roles and are able to work well on a team. In fact, with your empathetic, friendly nature, you have the ability to make others feel like family. You also have a great ability to understand complex issues and organizational problems and find workable solutions. On the other hand, you are inclined to overwork yourself, and you expect everyone else to do likewise. Everyone thinks you're such a money magnet, but they don't realize how hard you work for everything you have.

Best Trait: You persevere even in the worst situations.

Your Space: Your favorite room is the living room, where you like to get together and entertain family and friends. You prefer Danish modern decor, where simple, unadorned beauty and artfulness go hand in hand. You like to redecorate but have a hard time deciding where to hang that special picture. Your front yard is a masterpiece of landscaping, at least as long as you can keep the dog out of it.

Career: Do not squander your talents! You are a self-motivated person who can perform extremely well in jobs that require concentration. You'd have been a wonderful surgeon, if only you could stand the sight of blood. Perhaps you would do best as an administrative assistant, or even go into business for yourself. In any case, you need a job where you will not be scrutinized every second of the day and where you can use your abilities to work closely with others.

Leisure Time and Entertainment: For serious reading, you enjoy (or at least appreciate!) the works of the Danish philosopher Søren Kierkegaard—his theories on theology and ethics appeal to your ability to comprehend complex issues. For lighter reading, you enjoy romantic mysteries, such as works by Nora Roberts. For out and out laughter, you like the observational humor of Dane Cook. You are fond of the works of fellow Great Dane owner Andy Warhol; you understand that his art is a lot more complex than it may appear at first glance.

When it comes to vacation, Germany or Denmark are the obvious places—but there's so much more to the world! Consider talking a walking tour of parts of Europe. Bring your camera and your journal, and explore ancient castles and modern monuments. You need the time to unwind and get in touch with your inner self.

Fashion Musts: Your preferred clothing style is somewhat informal but still feminine and sexy. Whether going out to dinner with a date or having drinks with friends, you like to mix up modern and vintage looks—try a floral dress by Jill Stuart with a striking accessory, like a jeweled headband, to complete the look.

Food Faves: Even though Great Danes are from Germany, you still prefer Danish foods like herring and sausages. Try a big, traditional Danish meal comprising three or four courses, featuring meatballs made from a half-and-half mixture of chopped pork and chopped veal, mixed with egg, flour, liquid (milk or water), and salt and pepper. There's nothing quite like it!

Significant Others: You tend to be a flirt and exert a powerful sexual charisma. You can switch from sweet romance to fiery passion in about a minute and a half. Sometimes you're impulsive in your affections and tend to throw caution to the winds—and indulge in a little too much drama. You have a hard time saying no to your significant other, and that can be part of the problem. But on the whole, you enjoy a very rewarding romantic life.

Other Compatible Breed Personalities: Besides the Great Dane, you are compatible with mixed breeds and Vizslas.

Pet Peeve: You're bothered by people who shirk their responsibilities.

Lucky Number: Numerological calculations for your breed reveal your lucky number to be 3.

Notable Great Dane People: Brad Anderson, Jim Carey, Bruce Lee, Olivia Newton-John, Andy Warhol

Cultured and Classic

Irish Setter People

Personality and Character: You have a fascinating personality that combines respectability, sober energy, and utter abandon in a unique way. On one hand, you are a very peaceful person—cooperative, patient, and kind. You have deep feelings of compassion for those less fortunate and are quick to aid anyone in a time of trouble; you also have a special concern for those who are victims of prejudice. Generous beyond measure, you are willing to share almost anything you own. On the other hand, you get excited by new ideas and revel in new experiences. For example, you may "disappear" for the weekend without telling your coworkers, or in some cases, even your family, what you are up to. You are also very interested in how things work (especially if they save you time); indeed, you are in constant search for knowledge. You are also a tad nosy—and you can be a bit of a hypochondriac as well.

Best Trait: Your best trait is your generous nature.

Your Space: When it comes to home decor, you like to decorate with just a few large, solid pieces of furniture. (You have a preference for cherry wood.) Leather and wool are your favorite furniture fabrics. In pleasant weather, your favorite place is the porch—it's always nice to know what the neighbors are up to!

Career: A career that offers a lot of stability is best for you. You're a hard worker who doesn't mind working overtime, as long as the salary is good and the benefits generous, especially as concerns vacation time. Look for a job in the civil service, where you can help the needy.

Leisure Time and Entertainment: You enjoy reading the works of the great Irish writers like James Joyce and William Butler Yeats, and you have a considerable ability to write limericks. Musically, you have a beautiful voice and aren't shy about performing for a crowd. In your leisure time, you like small bookstores, out-of-the-way coffeehouses, and the beach at sunset, all quietly stimulating places that can be enjoyed with your significant other.

For vacation, you enjoy kicking back and being pampered. A health resort is a perfect place to recharge, and it wouldn't hurt if it were in Europe, especially Ireland. Select a place that offers aromatherapy, reflexology, energy bodywork, kinesiology, and rebirthing. You might as well try everything! Just don't pick a place that skimps on meals.

Fashion Musts: You have wonderful coloring, so highlight it with bold, shiny accessories like a chunky jeweled bracelet or pair of earrings. Where clothing is concerned, you often prefer natural woven pieces—you understand the importance of good craftsmanship. For a thoroughly modern look, don skinny jeans with a tunic top and a great pair of Christian Louboutin flats. One of your best physical traits is your smiling eyes, so accentuate them with a contrasting eye shadow or liner.

Food Faves: Like the Irish, you have a fondness for meat, potatoes, and butter. Luckily (and you are great believer in luck), your restless energy works it all off. This is a good thing, because you can really polish off two or even three bowls of Irish stew without taking a second breath. You also love your beer!

Significant Others: You tend to become deeply emotionally attached and deeply hurt when things go wrong. Trust your instincts, but don't get involved with those who have a record of hopping from one relationship to another—you could be next. You require a stable, committed person who will support you emotionally.

Other Compatible Breed Personalities: Besides the Irish Setter, you are compatible with Beagles and Saint Bernards.

Pet Peeve: You hate it when people are selfish.

Lucky Number: Numerological calculations for your breed reveal your lucky number to be 6.

Notable Irish Setter People: Erma Bombeck, Olivia Newton-John, Margaret Truman

Neapolitan Mastiff People

Personality and Character: You are highly intelligent and inventive. Steady and loyal, you are normally a person of penetrating judgment, more guided by reason than by feelings. You are capable of analyzing any situation quickly and making a quick decision regarding it. Knowledge is important to you, and you have an incredible curiosity about all things. You really have no patience with the "old way" of doing things and adapt to new situations with ease. Your biggest struggle is the age-old opposition between what your head and heart are telling you to do—you feel very torn at times. Some Neapolitan Mastiff people are obsessed with money, big houses, and material things; if this is you, it may be time to rethink your goals.

Best Trait: Your best trait is your ability to cope with almost any situation—usually by being prepared for it.

Your Space: Your home features a streamlined, ultra-modern look, and you take great care in making it look lovely, especially your living room, which is truly your creative retreat. (You also like to impress company.) Often you start out just wanting to add one stunning abstract picture or one exotic piece, and pretty soon you are redoing the whole house. You are also careful to paint your rooms a neutral color that camouflages drool well.

Career: A career in the law field would suit your analytical mind. You might also investigate a career in science or engineering. Try to find a job that allows you to think deeply as well as creatively.

Your Inner Dog

Leisure Time and Entertainment: When it comes to sports, you're a huge baseball and NASCAR fan. You also love tales of dragons, fair maidens, and hopeless romance, but then who doesn't? The Harry Potter movie series is one of your all-time favorites. (Hagrid's dog Fang, as you know, was played by a Neapolitan.) One of your favorite holidays is Halloween, but you don't always wear a costume—with the dog you have, you don't need to. A few of you have picked up some unusual and possibly frightening (to those who aren't familiar with them) hobbies, like snake keeping.

For vacation, what could be better than Naples itself? Either Naples, Florida, or Naples, Italy, will suit. It all depends on whether you are in the mood for beaches or volcanoes.

Fashion Musts: Like your home design, your personal style is modern, streamlined, and fashion forward. You love designers like Issey Miyake who use innovative techniques and fabrics to construct the perfect piece. The one thing that may not be the most fashion forward is your hair; if you've worn it the same way for longer than you care to admit, it's time for a change! Try a geometric bob or angled layers to create extra dimension to your look.

Food Faves: Sometimes you think you added a Neapolitan to the family just because you love Neapolitan cuisine. Favorites include Neapolitan ice cream, or in lighter moods, a simple gelato. Naples is the traditional home of rich, savory pizza, and you can't get enough of it, diet be darned! Your favorite is the Neapolitan margherita, cooked in a wood-burning oven. Spaghetti with a ragu sauce is also so you. You love Vesuvius wines and the ever-popular lemon liqueur.

Significant Others: When you fall in love, you tend to lose the clear reasoning that guides you most of the time. You make the mistake of spending everything you have to impress your new squeeze, but that is really not necessary. You also have a habit of falling for people who you just met—spend some time to get to know them better. Take a more sensible approach and look for someone with whom you have common interests, especially someone who appreciates beauty and the finer things in life—like your dog. (Not everyone has the power to appreciate how gorgeous your drooling hunk really is.)

Other Compatible Breed Personalities: Besides the Neapolitan Mastiff, you are compatible with Pembroke Welsh Corgis and Rhodesian Ridgebacks.

Pet Peeve: People who soak themselves in cologne make you crazy.

Lucky Number: Numerological calculations for your breed reveal your lucky number to be 6.

Notable Neapolitan Mastiff People: Alexander the Great, Gillian Anderson, Hagrid, Kate Hudson

Personality and Character: Sweetness of temperament, sensitivity, self-control, and strong humanitarian values are the hallmarks of your character. You also have a wonderful sense of humor, and honor is extremely important to you. You are known for your prudence and practicality, as well as for your sensitivity to others (even so far as feeling a need to "rescue" them). You are truly the champion of lost causes. You work extremely hard and would rather "do it all" yourself than ask others to share the burden; in fact, you dislike interference, although you are diplomatic about keeping others out of your way. You have superior organizational abilities, and your hard work usually pays off. On the downside, you can be extremely stubborn at times, wedded to your own way of doing things; this can get you stuck in a rut if you're not careful.

Best Trait: You have a willingness to just dive in there and rescue people.

Your Space: Your ideal home is an old farmhouse that you can fix up and make your own. You wouldn't mind in the least if it has a reputation for being haunted; in fact, you'd rather enjoy the experience. Your favorite room is the garage, or more accurately, your workshop in the garage. In the garden, you have a preference for the native plants of Newfoundland, including ferns, pitcher plants, certain orchids, and blueberries.

Career: Newfie people would often rather work behind the scenes instead of being the center of attention. Because you are diplomatic, well organized, and have excellent communication skills, you would excel as a teacher, therapist, or public relations person. You would also do well in humanitarian work.

Leisure Time and Entertainment: You enjoy comedies of all kinds, for you like to laugh. Romantic novels are also great favorites. Because you are a talented dancer as well as a good swimmer, consider combining your skills—try synchronized swimming! As far as music goes, some Newfie people are actually a little tone deaf and only use it for background noise.

When it comes to vacation, Newfie people love to explore different cultures, but they are just as happy using their vacation time taking a special class in photography or art. This makes you feel more well rounded and complete. Inner peace is more important than taking a trip (and usually cheaper!). A thrifty person, you are also likely to spend your free time shopping for hidden treasures at a local flea market or yard sale.

Fashion Musts: Your personal style is elegant and understated. Rather than shopping for trendy clothing that will go out of style within a few months, you prefer to find timeless pieces that serve you well for years. The label St. John Knits is one of your favorites, and not just because St. John's (the capital of Newfoundland/Labrador and the oldest city in North America) is in your dog's neck of the woods. You appreciate its quality fabrics and classic designs, especially when it comes to evening wear.

Food Faves: You would like to honor your breed's Newfoundland heritage—where people have lived and died for cod—by being partial to codfish, but unfortunately, it's not one of your favorites. You do, however, have a soft spot for the Newfie version of figgy duff around Christmastime, a delicious breadcrumb, molasses, and raisin pudding. For additional traditional fare, try the native Newfoundland stew made of salt beef, cabbage, carrots, turnips, and potatoes.

Significant Others: When it comes to relationships, you sometimes tend to be attracted to those who are too busy and restless to provide the support you need. Your biggest danger is your constant need to "rescue" people. This is fine for ordinary friendships, but it's not the best basis on which to build a life partnership. Look for someone who is steadfast and calm—and who can support *you* during the rare times you need rescuing yourself.

Other Compatible Breed Personalities: Besides the Newfoundland, you are compatible with English Springer Spaniels and Great Pyrenees.

Pet Peeve: You're bothered by spendthrifts and people who don't understand the value of money.

Lucky Number: Numerological calculations for your breed reveal your lucky number to be 7.

Notable Newfoundland People: J.M. Barrie, Lord Byron, Emily Dickinson, Ulysses S. Grant, Meriwether Lewis

Cultured and Classic

Personality and Character: Warmhearted, original, and optimistic, you wish to bring joy to all. Although you are a born leader, you are respectful and supportive of others, with a terrific ability to motivate. People rely on your common sense and follow your advice. Generally, you are of a peaceable nature, but when challenged, you can become extremely argumentative. If called upon to fight in a righteous cause, you will do so, and you are very straightforward in all your dealings. When you want something, you go after it with a fierce determination, and you will sacrifice anything to get what you truly want. You need to be careful that in your optimistic haste to accomplish something, you don't overlook a critical detail. You also have a stubborn streak; you form your convictions early and are not inclined to change them. You would do better to listen carefully, learn to read between the lines, and compromise where necessary.

Best Trait: You always stand up for what you believe to be right.

Your Space: You love every inch of your home, and you are constantly redecorating in search of the perfect ambience. You are so orderly, and your house is so well decorated, that your friends remark on it. You love to change the look of a room by painting the walls different shades of cool colors like greens and blues, and you especially love wall murals.

Your Inner Dog

Career: You make a better boss than an employee because you are able to anticipate problems and see the big picture. You work best in flexible careers where you can be fully creative. Writing, broadcasting, and administration are all good possibilities.

Leisure Time and Entertainment: You love reading classic English novelists like Thomas Hardy, Jane Austen, and Charles Dickens—and the longer the book, the better you like it. You're also a fan of art that features your breed, such as the superb portrait of two old English Sheepdogs by Edwin Megargee. You also love to drive; after all, the Old English Sheepdog is a "drover" of sheep!

When it comes to vacation, you view travel as a chance to escape from your everyday life. You like to try new foods, see new sights, and experience the culture of the area you are visiting. If you can come home with some exotic trinkets from your travels, even better! Consider visiting a resort island like Bali or Tahiti—soak up the experiences as well as the sun.

Fashion Musts: Your personal style involves wearing the latest trends—you like to stand out from the crowd. Mixing and matching seemingly incongruous pieces, like label Sass & Bide is renowned for, is your trademark. For example, you might pair a sparkly minidress with chunky work boots or add menswear touches to an otherwise ultrafeminine piece. Some of your best colors include golds, oranges, and reds.

Food Faves: Chocolate trifle, Yorkshire pudding, and other classically English dishes are your favorites. They may not be the world's healthiest foods, but they are delicious and life is short!

Significant Others: You are charming and can win hearts with your smile alone. Look for a quiet, reserved partner to complement your personality, preferably not someone in the same field as yourself. (Things could get too competitive.) With the right partner, you will be very successful and prosperous in your relationship.

Other Compatible Breed Personalities: Besides the Old English Sheepdog, you are compatible with Basset Hounds and Bloodhounds

Pet Peeve: Your biggest pet peeve is people who chew gum loud enough to be heard across the street.

Lucky Number: Numerological calculations for your breed reveal your lucky number to be 1.

Notable Old English Sheepdog People: Joan Van Ark, Lynn Johnston, Paul McCartney, Franklin D. Roosevelt, Katharine Ross

Cultured and Classic

Saluki People

Personality and Character: You are a friendly, popular person and have many friends—and you are especially fond of children. You are also interested in issues of justice and equality, and you are deeply concerned with the issue of humanity's destiny. It is your nature to assume responsibility, although this same trait can cause you to be anxious and short-tempered at times. You are supersensitive emotionally, but physically you are incredibly tough. You are also deeply intuitive, rather than cerebral, although you sometimes use your amazing powers of insight to coerce and manipulate others. Some of you tend to live in a fantasy world, as you can quickly become bored in this one.

Best Trait: You are able to truly understand what people are feeling.

Your Space: You love wide-open areas, both inside and out. Your home is noted for its fine carpets and lovely red and gold accents. It is definitely uncluttered, exotic, and beautiful. One of your favorite spaces is outside in your garden with your herbs. You like to imagine that some of them are just a little bit magical, and only you know how to charm them.

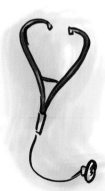

Career: Able, aware, and ethical, you are best suited to working alone, even if your job is with a large company. You do best in specialized rather than general positions. You can excel in health care, investigative journalism, psychology, law, and business.

Leisure Time and Entertainment: You love music (you sing well) and dance, and you are also an excellent gardener. When it comes to books, there's nothing better than fantasy literature, especially the *Lord of the Rings* trilogy. You also enjoy art that features your favorite breed, such as the Saluki portrait of Zillah, by English painter Charles Hamilton.

Most Saluki people are rather homebodies when it comes to vacation, preferring the allure of the garden to some extravagant vacation far away. You like to keep up with your hobbies, especially when it comes to fixing up the house. (Besides, your active imagination provides you plenty of places to go.) If you do decide to take a trip, consider heading for wide-open spaces and do a little rock climbing and hiking—and perhaps pick up some new and unusual plants.

Fashion Musts: You have a fabulous figure and like to show it off in clothes that flow on the body—especially glamorous evening gowns. For a special occasion, try a Marc Bouwer dress; his line features imaginative, form-fitting pieces in beautiful fabrics like silk and cashmere. You'll feel like royalty!

Food Faves: Desserts of all kinds are your favorite—chocolate cake, candy bars, ice cream, pie—although you try not to overindulge. You balance your dessert addiction with healthier meals that feature lots of fruits, veggies, and whole grains. You have to maintain that svelte figure somehow!

Significant Others: You are a devoted partner and are also extremely involved with your siblings and children, who mean a great deal to you. Look for someone who values independence but who also enjoys spending time with you; in other words, choose someone who likes to be together but who isn't too clingy.

Other Compatible Breed Personalities: Besides the Saluki, you are compatible with Brittanys and West Highland White Terriers.

Pet Peeve: It drives you crazy when people just won't listen to facts.

Lucky Number: Numerological calculations for your breed reveal your lucky number to be 1.

Notable Saluki People: Emperor Frederick II of Sicily, Lady Florence Amherst

Personality and Character: You are well known for your excellent, if somewhat acerbic, communication skills. While in some ways you are a creature of habit, you are also admired for your determination and resourcefulness. Your positive thinking as far as business and career are concerned is legendary. You are a fighter from the word go, and people admire you for it. Life is not worth living for you unless you are doing something, and you keep up with the latest technology so that you can multitask. In your relations with others, you can be somewhat dogmatic, and when you say something, you mean it. Your single-mindedness sometimes affects your manners, and you are rather frequently at odds with your family and friends. If you can learn to admit when you are wrong, you will find that things will go a lot more easily in your life.

Best Trait: You have a lot of positive energy.

Your Space: You like decorating in shades of red, but be careful not to go overboard on this dramatic color. One single dramatic piece, such as the front door or living room carpet, is enough. Stay away from florals—they're not really you. Your ideal home has multiple floors, with a great patio for the outdoor living you so admire.

Career: You would make an innovative and entrepreneurial businessperson. You are also good at science and math, so consider a career that plays to these strengths.

Leisure Time and Entertainment: You're a huge football fan—and you give the best Super Bowl

Your Inner Dog

party on the block! You also like baseball, skiing, tennis, golf, and chess. Your restless energy makes you crave excitement and competition, whether you are participating or just watching. Your favorite entertainers include Drew Barrymore, the Gabor sisters, Paul Newman, Goldie Hawn, and Tony Curtis—Hungarians all, just like your Vizsla.

When it comes to vacation, there's nothing like Las Vegas—just be careful not to lose all your money! You might also consider a visit to the motherland, so to speak: Hungary.

Fashion Musts: If left to your own devices, you tend to wear the same style of clothing over and over—but your style is very clean and simple, so you always look great. One of your favorite designers is Yves St. Laurent—the label's power suits match you perfectly. When it comes to makeup, try a bold red on the lips to enhance the rest of your ensemble, but be sure to choose just the right shade! Your hair color is wonderful—don't let your hairdresser talk you into changing it.

Food Faves: Just as you love your Hungarian dog, so do you love Hungarian foods: goulash, chicken paprika, and anything with onions. Try Hungarian sausage, a real delicacy.

Significant Others: You are attracted to smart, honest people with a sense of humor. However, you need someone who is willing to tolerate your passion to always be doing something. You're not a romantic, so you don't expect flowers and chocolates.

Other Compatible Breed Personalities: Besides the Vizsla, you are compatible with Great Danes and mixed breeds.

Pet Peeve: The weather, no matter what it is—it's never quite right for you.

Lucky Number: Numerological calculations for your breed reveal your lucky number to be 8.

Notable Vizsla People: William Fox, Seal

Personality and Character: You are a risk taker and a quick reactor, and you enjoy a fast-paced, active lifestyle. You're a fast mover, thinker, and talker who hates routine and gets bored easily. (Sometimes you even try to be in two places at once.) You desire to excel in all your endeavors. You are idealistic, intelligent, assertive, and outspoken, a true leader with many admirers. You dislike details but need to pay attention to them if you are going to succeed—and you do have big, big plans. On the downside, you can be detached at times and sometimes overlook important matters because you're so busy doing a hundred other things. In fact, tension often seems to surround you, but in most situations, no one could be more warmhearted and generous. Overall, it's important for you to focus on things that are really within your control and not waste your incredible energy on things that aren't.

Best Trait: You have a tremendous gift for self-expression, and most people find you fascinating.

Your Space: You value comfort above all else when it comes to your living space. In fact, the Weim person doesn't usually put a lot of effort into home decor—you're happier hanging out in a shabby but comfortable chair. However, "hanging out" is a bit of an exaggeration. The truth is that you don't spend enough time at home to worry about what it looks like. You probably don't even know what color rug you have—you have many more important things to do. You have a strong connection to nature, and so you love to be outside, especially in places with spectacular views.

Career: You have a tendency to change careers relatively often because you're easily bored and always on the lookout for something new. Considering your penchant for new things, look for a career that takes you to different places, such as photojournalism (perhaps its the Wegman influence!). If that doesn't pan out, you are such a quick learner that you can change fields with little difficulty. The only problem is that you often don't stick at one thing long enough to rise to the very top.

Leisure Time and Entertainment: You really enjoy socializing with your friends, and you are so funny and charming that you have a great many of them. You also like loud parties, extreme sports, and even amateur theatre. You like a lot of movies, but *Best in Show* is not one of them. (You know that Weimaraners are nothing like the way Beatrice was portrayed.) While you are not a huge reader of fiction, you do enjoy collecting travel guides as well as mystery, crime, and ghost stories. All of them help satisfy your need for thrills.

For vacation, take a trip to Weimar, Germany, just for the fun of it—you certainly don't want to miss the annual onion festival in Thuringia. When not honoring your dog's roots, you like to live on the edge and prefer an action-filled getaway like an African safari or canoeing in British Columbia.

Fashion Musts: When it comes to fashion, you have the gift of uniting the unpretentious with the completely becoming. Every once in a while, you indulge your taste for the theatrical—perhaps a floor length faux-fur coat or a flowing gown paired with a simple head scarf. For a designer look, try something by John Galliano, who manages to merge glamour and theatrics in his wonderfully constructed pieces.

Food Faves: You like to explore a lot of variety in your food and prefer buffets, where you can try a little bit of everything! For the same reason, you love tapas and often frequent tapas bars. There is very little food that you don't like, actually, but you never gorge on anything.

Significant Others: In a relationship, you definitely need attention and affection, and you deserve someone who will supply it. Be careful, as you can be manipulative, unpredictable, and even fickle. You are also very protective of your significant other, sometimes too much so.

Other Compatible Breed Personalities: Besides the Weimaraner, you are compatible with Boxers and Siberian Huskies.

Pet Peeve: You hate not receiving enough credit for your efforts.

Lucky Number: Numerological calculations for your breed reveal your lucky number to be 4.

Notable Weimaraner People: Dean Cain, Dwight D. Eisenhower, Brad Pitt, Trent Reznor, William Wegman

Resources

Breed Clubs

American Kennel Club (AKC)
5580 Centerview Drive
Raleigh, NC 27606
Telephone: (919) 233-9767
Fax: (919) 233-3627
E-mail: info@akc.org
www.akc.org

Canadian Kennel Club (CKC)
89 Skyway Avenue, Suite 100
Etobicoke, Ontario M9W 6R4
Telephone: (416) 675-5511
Fax: (416) 675-6506
E-mail: information@ckc.ca
www.ckc.ca

Federation Cynologique Internationale (FCI)
Secretariat General de la FCI
Place Albert 1er, 13
B – 6530 Thuin
Belqique
www.fci.be

The Kennel Club
1 Clarges Street
London
W1J 8AB
Telephone: 0870 606 6750
Fax: 0207 518 1058
www.the-kennel-club.org.uk

United Kennel Club (UKC)
100 E. Kilgore Road
Kalamazoo, MI 49002-5584
Telephone: (269) 343-9020
Fax: (269) 343-7037
E-mail: pbickell@ukcdogs.com
www.ukcdogs.com

Rescue Organizations and Animal Welfare Groups

American Humane Association (AHA)
63 Inverness Drive East
Englewood, CO 80112
Telephone: (303) 792-9900
Fax: 792-5333
www.americanhumane.org

American Society for the Prevention of Cruelty to Animals (ASPCA)
424 E. 92nd Street
New York, NY 10128-6804
Telephone: (212) 876-7700
www.aspca.org

Royal Society for the Prevention of Cruelty to Animals (RSPCA)
Telephone: 0870 3335 999
Fax: 0870 7530 284
www.rspca.org.uk

The Humane Society of the United States (HSUS)
2100 L Street, NW
Washington DC 20037
Telephone: (202) 452-1100
www.hsus.org

Websites

Nylabone
www.nylabone.com

T.F.H. Publications, Inc.
www.tfh.com

Gone 2 the Dogs
Take a ten-question quiz to find out what kind of dog you are.
http://www.gone2thedogs.com/

iVillage.co.uk
This seven-question quiz will tell you what kind of dog you are.
http://quiz.ivillage.co.uk/uk_astrology/tests/dogs.htm

The What Breed of Dog Are You Test
Take a 17-question test to find out what breed of dog you'd be.
http://www.okcupid.com/tests/take?testid=15523834815
565088491

Index

Note: **Boldfaced** numbers indicate main discussion for breed profiles.

Dedication

For Jamie and Sunny Garcia, in grateful recognition of all their efforts on behalf of homeless animals.

Acknowledgements

My deepest thanks to Stephanie Fornino, editor nonpareil at T.F.H., for taking this manuscript firmly in hand and managing to transform it. The quiz at the beginning of the book is her work. I am also in deepest gratitude to Heather Russell-Revesz for her creative and funny suggestions. You guys are the very best.

About the Author

Diane Morgan teaches philosophy and comparative religion at Wilson College. She has authored numerous books on canine care and nutrition and has also written many breed books. Her style sense is inspired by Target and Goodwill. Her food faves include anything of high caloric content. (She didn't arrive at her current size by being picky.) Her favorite room is the great outdoors—even with all the dirt out there, it never needs dusting. Diane lives in Williamsport, Maryland, with several dogs.

Photo Credits

Utekhina Anna (Shutterstock): 10 (bottom), 27, 48, 99, 131, 138 (bottom), 140, 152, 160
Annette (Shutterstock): 9 (bottom), 11 (far left), 21, 65, 139 (far left), 143
arfo (Shutterstock): 104
Répási Lajos Attila (Shutterstock): front cover, 1
Jessica Bilén (Shutterstock): 162
Anthony Bolan (Shutterstock): 83
emmanuelle bonzami (Shutterstock): 57
Joy Brown (Shutterstock): 142, 144
Norman Chan (Shutterstock): 88
Lars Christensen (Shutterstock): 139 (middle), 155
Perry Correll (Shutterstock): 93
Candice M Cunningham (Shutterstock): 8 (top)
Waldemar Dabrowski (Shutterstock): 30, 58, 148
Jeff Dalton (Shutterstock): 122
Phil Date (Shutterstock): 42 (bottom), 75 (middle)
Tad Denson (Shutterstock): 79, 138 (top), 161
Julie DeGuia (Shutterstock): 17
digitalsport-photoagency (Shutterstock): 75 (far right)
Boulatov Dmitry (Shutterstock): 90
Mindaugas Dulinskas (Shutterstock): 156
Jaime Duplass (Shutterstock): 9 (middle)
John Evans (Shutterstock): 126
Darren K. Fisher (Shutterstock): 38
Cate Frost (Shutterstock): 130
Karen Givens (Shutterstock): 78
Hannamariah (Shutterstock): 43 (middle), 49
Geoff Hardy (Shutterstock): 18

Margo Harrison (Shutterstock): 116
Andrew Howard (Shutterstock): 123
Aleksey Ignatenko (Shutterstock): 40, 84
ingret (Shutterstock): 25
iofoto (Shutterstock): 61, 121, 149
Moyseeva Irina (Shutterstock): 41
Eric Isselée (Shutterstock): 11 (far right), 15, 23, 19, 29, 31, 39, 43 (far right), 73, 75 (far left), 77, 85, 91, 95, 103, 105, 115, 127, 139 (far right), 145, 151, 163
JD (Shutterstock): 72
Gary Jones (Shutterstock): 128
Judy Ben Joud (Shutterstock): 114, 165
Laila Kazakevica (Shutterstock): 56, 136
Cynthia Kidwell (Shutterstock): 120
Dmitry Kosterev (Shutterstock): 118
Nadezhda V. Kulagina (Shutterstock): 8 (bottom)
Erik Lam (Shutterstock): 59 (right), 81, 101, 119, 135, 153
michael ledray (Shutterstock): 13
laurie lindstrom (Shutterstock): 146
Shane Wilson Link (Shutterstock): 26
luchschen (Shutterstock): 9 (top)
Dwight Lyman (Shutterstock): 168
Kaleb Madsen (Shutterstock): 52
Tommy Maenhout (Shutterstock): 54
Dina Magnat (Shutterstock): 141
MalibuBooks (Shutterstock): 36
Theresa Martinez (Shutterstock): 112
Suponev Vladimir Mihajlovich (Shutterstock): 35
Clara Natoli (Shutterstock): 94
ncn18 (Shutterstock): 110
Kerioak-Christine Nichols (Shutterstock): 86, 87, 167
Iztoc Noc (Shutterstock): 62, 132
Rhonda ODonnell (Shutterstock): 113

Pieter (Shutterstock): 55
pixshots (Shutterstock): 33
plastique (Shutterstock): 134
Tatiana Popova (Shutterstock): 32
Shirelle Reggio-Manning: 51
Nicholas Rjabow (Shutterstock): 74 (bottom)
Josh Rodriguez (Shutterstock): 28
stephen rudolph (Shutterstock): 12
Rena Schild (Shutterstock): 157
Jennifer Sekerka (Shutterstock): 74 (top)
Sergey I (Shutterstock): 111, 154
Shutterstock: 37, 53, 69, 71, 166
Nikola Spasenoski (Shutterstock): 102
Nikolay Starchenko (Shutterstock): 98
Susan Stayer (Shutterstock): 10 (top)
Claudia Steininger (Shutterstock): 80, 108, 150
Konstantin Sutyagin (Shutterstock): 24
MAGDALENA SZACHOWSKA (Shutterstock): 89, 137
Nikita Tiunov (Shutterstock): 42 (top)
Nikolai Tsvetkov (Shutterstock): 22
Hedser van Brug (Shutterstock): 164
vnlit (Shutterstock): 106 (top), 109
Elliott Westacott (Shutterstock): 63 (left)
WizData, inc. (Shutterstock): 11 (middle), 34
Jeffrey Ong Guo Xiong (Shutterstock): 64, 107 (far left)
Lisa F. Young (Shutterstock): 20
Ryhor M Zasinets (Shutterstock): 82

All other photos courtesy of Isabelle Francais, T.F.H. archives, and Nylabone. Illustrations courtesy of Stephanie Krautheim, with the exception of pages 17 (top), 18, 31 (bottom), and 80.

Nylabone Cares.

Dogs of all ages, breeds, and sizes have enjoyed our world-famous chew bones for over 50 years. For the safest, healthiest, and happiest lifetime your dog can possibly have, choose from a variety of Nylabone® Pet Products!

Toys

Treats

Chews

Crates

Grooming

Available at retailers everywhere. Visit us online at www.nylabone.com